# How To Profit by

# Forming Your Own Limited Liability Company

## SCOTT E. FRIEDMAN

UPSTART PUBLISHING
*Specializing in Small Business Publishing*
a division of Dearborn Publishing Group, Inc.

# Dedication

This book is dedicated to my wife, Lisa, and my children, Samantha, Eliza, Julia and Madeline; my parents, Iris and Irwin Friedman; and my parents-in-law, Sylvia and Irwin Pastor.

Executive Editor: Bobbye Middendorf
Managing Editor: Jack Kiburz
Associate Project Editor: Stephanie C. Schmidt
Interior Design: Lucy Jenkins
Cover Design: The Publishing Services Group

© 1996 by Scott E. Friedman

Published by Upstart Publishing Company, Inc.,
a division of Dearborn Publishing Group, Inc.

Printed in the United States of America

96 97 98 10 9 8 7 6 5 4 3 2

**Library of Congress Cataloging-in-Publication Data**

Friedman, Scott E., 1958—
    How to profit by forming your own limited liability company / by Scott E. Friedman.
        p.  cm.
    Includes index.
    ISBN 0-936894-93-8
    1. Private companies—United States—Popular works. 2. Private
companies—Taxation—United States—Popular works. 3. Tax planning—
United States—Popular works. I. Title.
KF1380.Z9F75  1995
346.73 0668—dc20                                               95-18580
[347.30 6668]                                                        CIP

# Contents

# Preface

It is not unusual for changes to take place in the law. Every day, legislation is enacted and cases that serve as precedents are decided by our judiciary. These changes may range from minor to significant. A very few changes are so important that they can best be described as "revolutionary." Because revolutionary changes are so rare, it is exciting when they do occur and a privilege to be able to help spread the news.

I believe the subject of this book—limited liability companies or, as they are often called, LLCs—is a revolutionary subject, one that promises to reshape the business landscape throughout the United States. Let me offer a brief background to help place this exciting new subject in perspective.

Any entrepreneur who is either thinking about starting a business or is already in business has to decide what the "form" of the business should be or whether to change to another form. Historically, the choice has largely been between sole proprietorships, partnerships and corporations.

In making this selection, entrepreneurs had to weigh the advantages of these various business forms against their disadvantages. One set of disadvantages could be offset by selecting an alternative business form only to find other disadvantages. For example, an entrepreneur can establish an S corporation as a shield against personal liability but, by doing so, is restricted from creating common and preferred stock, since this form of corporation can issue only one class of stock.

Because of the varying characteristics of traditional business forms, an entrepreneur often was forced to decide which characteristics to secure and which to sacrifice. Thus, securing the benefits of limited liability offered by a corporate form of business meant foregoing the simplicity of the noncorporate forms and perhaps being subject to an additional level of income tax. To achieve simplicity and avoid this double tax, another possibility was to forego the limited liability protection offered by a corporate business form and, instead, operate as a proprietorship or, if the entrepreneur could qualify, an S corporation. The opportunity cost of each business form would usually require an expensive and time-consuming analysis by a business attorney or accountant, who could then recommend the best (or the least troublesome) form of business for that entrepreneur.

As a result, many businesses change their forms as they grow and evolve. For example, many businesses are established by individual entrepreneurs operating as sole proprietorships. Over time, the proprietor might seek the assistance of one or more partners and convert to a partnership. Later, the partnership may be converted into an S corporation and, thereafter (perhaps if the business goes public), it becomes a C corporation.

In 1977, Wyoming took a gigantic step forward by enacting a statute permitting the establishment of limited liability companies. LLCs combine the advantages of the noncorporate forms of business with the advantages of the corporate forms. The result: A revolutionary hybrid form of business that many experts predict will become the business form of choice for most new businesses.

The LLC went largely unnoticed in the business and legal community until 1988. In that year, the IRS issued Revenue Ruling 88-76, which concluded that a Wyoming LLC could be classified as a partnership for federal income tax purposes, even though its members were not personally liable for the debts of the company.

The IRS ruling began a movement throughout the country's statehouses that grew to virtual tidal-wave proportions in the past two years, with 18 states adopting LLC legislation in 1993 and 11 other states doing so in 1994. As of March 1995, LLC legislation has been adopted in 47 states and the District of Columbia. Only Hawaii, Massachusetts and Vermont have yet to authorize LLCs, although legislation which would do so has now been proposed in each of these states.

What is this new form of business all about? How is it set up and how does it work? How can it help you accomplish your business objectives cheaply and simply? Sit back, relax and read carefully (you'll find this book written in plain English!). To help you better understand the concepts discussed in this book—and to help you act on them—the book includes 140 planning tips that offer real-world suggestions. Also included are discussions of how John Smith, a fictitious entrepreneur, benefits from his use of an LLC. You'll find this part of the discussion under the heading Entrepreneurs in Action. By considering the text, planning tips and Entrepreneurs in Action examples—all of which approach the subject in slightly different ways—the overall picture will become much clearer to you. I have included these sections in hopes that you can more easily learn how this revolution in the U.S. legal system may help you profit by forming your own limited liability company.

Because the creation of LLCs is so new, some of the legal issues discussed in this book rapidly are being clarified. I would love to hear from you and learn what your experience with an LLC has been. If you have additional thoughts or ideas on how LLCs can be used for other purposes, I'd love to hear them as well. You can contact me at my office in Buffalo:

| By Telephone | By Fax | By Mail |
|---|---|---|
| 716-853-5100 | 716-853-5199 | Lippes, Silverstein, Mathias & Wexler, LLP 28 Church St. 700 Guaranty Building Buffalo, NY 14202 |

I look forward to learning how *you* have profited by forming your own limited liability company!

## Acknowledgments

In my previous books, I have saved the customary acknowledgment of my wife and children for the end. I now depart from that custom and thank my wife, Lisa, and my children, Samantha, Eliza, Julia and Madeline, for permitting me the time, and providing me with the support and encouragement, to complete this book in a very short time. This book could only be completed thanks to their patience while I worked long and difficult hours. It is as much theirs as mine.

I would also like to thank my partners and colleagues at Lippes, Silverstein, Mathias & Wexler, LLP. It is a rare privilege to be a part of this team of professionals and, without their support, I could not have completed this book on schedule. Special thanks to my partner, Gerald S. Lippes, whose encouragement to undertake this project was so important to me, and to another one of my partners, Henry M. Porter, whose legal and business expertise provides a constant and fertile sounding board. Thanks also to Elaine W. Pauly for her helpful organizational suggestions.

Thanks to David R. Barrett, a partner in the Buffalo accounting firm Freed, Maxick, Sachs & Murphy, who reviewed my manuscript and made a number of helpful technical suggestions. Any mistakes, of course, remain mine.

Thanks to my secretary, Judy Kowalik, who managed to expertly type the manuscript by squeezing this project into her already busy days without any complaint.

Finally, thanks to everyone at Dearborn for assistance and support, particularly Bobbye Middendorf for her patience and editorial skills, as well as Jack Kiburz, Stephanie Schmidt and Lucy Jenkins. The challenge of writing this book was tolerable watching these experts guide it from stage to stage to stage and, finally, to publication.

# CHAPTER 1

# Overcoming the "Choice of Entity" Dilemma

The advantages of operating your business as an LLC are best illustrated by a comparison with the other traditional business forms, particularly proprietorships, partnerships and corporations. These traditional forms of business each offered features that were attractive to entrepreneurs. Nevertheless, each had substantial disadvantages as well. Because the LLC business form combines the best features of these business forms and gets rid of the worst, the future of business will be far different than its past.

### Planning Tip 1

The discussion that follows concentrates on the most commonly used forms of business. Other forms exist as well. Carefully consider all different business forms with an adviser before settling on one.

## Advantages of Proprietorships

Proprietorships provide their owners with a number of attractive features.

### Ease of Formation

A proprietorship is the simplest of all business forms as well as the easiest to set up. It is merely a business that is owned and operated by an individual. No special documentation is required to create a proprietorship. An entrepreneur opens for business and the proprietorship is underway. On occasion, some proprietors operate their businesses under fictitious names and need to file a "DBA" ("doing business as . . .") certificate with the local county clerk's office. It doesn't get too much more complicated than that.

### Pass-Through Tax Treatment

Proprietorships are also attractive because the business itself is not taxed on the income it earns. Instead, the income (or loss) generated by the business is passed through to the proprietor, who, in turn, reflects such income (or loss) on his or her personal tax return. The single level of tax imposed on a proprietor's income should be lower than that for an identical business formed as a corporation, since such a business would be responsible for an additional level of tax on income earned by the corporation and paid out as nondeductible dividends. If the proprietorship is fortunate, and incurs no extraordinary liability as a result of its activities, it may secure a competitive advantage over the corporation since it will have more available cash (since it pays less in taxes). If, however, the proprietorship unintentionally incurs such an extraordinary liability, the proprietor may be forced out of the business and have personal assets depleted.

# Disadvantages of Proprietorships

### Personal Liability

In spite of the ease of formation and low cost associated with proprietorships, this popular form of business has substantial disadvantages. Perhaps the biggest problem is that the business liabilities of the proprietorship are also the personal liabilities of the proprietor. What does that mean? Let's consider an example.

#### Entrepreneurs in Action

We'll call our proprietor John Smith. John opens a restaurant as a proprietorship, which is quite successful. After several years, he has managed to draw out $100,000 and it is now safely earning interest in one of his banks. He plans to use the money for daughter Jane's college education. One day, a patron slips on a wet floor, falls and breaks both legs. The patron's brother, an attorney, advises him to pursue his claim for damages against the restaurant as well as any of John's other assets. John's dream of using the money in the bank for his daughter's college education has suddenly become a nightmare! His savings are now at risk because a proprietor is personally liable for the debts of his or her business!

### Transferability of Ownership Interests

Sole proprietorships are also imperfect vehicles to transfer a business from an owner to other individuals. The assets and liabilities of the business can only be voluntarily transferred by sale, gift or, at death, by will. A proprietor who wishes to bring in another owner to help run the operation, perhaps a child who is interested in joining the family business, has no convenient tools to allow the transfer of an ownership interest without also transferring a degree of managerial authority (such as, for example, by use of nonvoting stock). Indeed, when a second owner joins the proprietorship, the business form is automatically converted into a partnership, even if that is not the result intended by the owners, since a proprietorship can only be owned by one individual. When a proprietor dies, the proprietorship terminates. If the heirs desire, they can establish a new business to succeed the proprietorship. This forced termination can cause confusion with customers, disruption in business operations and, ultimately, lost revenues.

## Advantages of General Partnerships

### Ease of Formation

A general partnership is a voluntary association of two or more individuals or business entities who agree to work together for a common business purpose. The partners, who own the business, share their profits or losses equally or as otherwise provided by agreement. Like proprietorships, partnerships can be formed easily. No formal steps are required to either establish or maintain a partnership. In order to confirm certain aspects of their relationship, many partners enter into a written partnership agreement to specify their understanding on matters such as how the profits and losses of the business should be allocated and procedures for admission of new partners and withdrawal of existing ones.

### Pass-Through Tax Treatment

Like proprietorships, partnerships offer business owners "pass-through" tax treatment. The partnership doesn't pay income tax. Instead, the income, profits, losses and expenses of the partnership flow directly through to the partners, who report their allocable share of income and expenses on their personal tax returns. Because partnership income is not taxed at the partnership level, operating a business as a partnership is, like a proprietorship, attractive from a tax perspective.

# Disadvantages of General Partnerships

## *Personal Liability*

What's the big problem with partnerships? You guessed it. Liability! In a general partnership, each partner is personally liable for all debts and obligations of the business. The consequences of this rule in a worst case scenario could prove disastrous. If one partner innocently (or negligently) makes a mistake, it could cost all the partners. The problem is especially significant because individual partners may be forced to satisfy the business obligation out of their personal assets if the business assets are inadequate.

### Entrepreneurs in Action

Consider what could happen if John Smith decides to bring in his brother-in-law, Mike Harris, as an equal partner in the restaurant business. John would like to open another shop and Mike has the financial resources that John lacks to make this dream a reality. They draw up a partnership agreement and begin working together. Mike, however, is a big spender. He buys a new company car for himself. Then he buys a new computer system for the business. Next, he buys TV advertisements at a cost of $30,000. When John learns of the ad campaign, he objects. He believes it's too expensive and the benefits are unclear. John calls the TV station to cancel the contract but, unfortunately for John, it's too late. As a partner in the business, Mike had authority to commit the business to the contract, and John is now bound by it. Worse, if the business defaults on its payment to the station, John can be sued for the debt and his personal resources (including Jane's college fund) are at risk.

## *Lack of Continuity*

Another problem with partnerships is that they lack business continuity. What do I mean? Without an agreement to the contrary, whenever an existing partner ceases to be a partner, whether as a result of retirement, death, expulsion or the like, the partnership ordinarily is deemed to have been dissolved as a matter of law. If Mike has a heart attack and dies, the business automatically terminates. Steps could be taken to continue the business, with or without one of Mike's heirs, but the process is not automatic. If Mike's heirs decide not to continue the business, they could require a distribution of partnership assets and force a liquidation of the business. All of John's hard work goes down the tubes!

### Lack of Investment Flexibility

General partnerships are financed either through capital contributions made by partners or by the use of debt. Although there is some flexibility to finance a general partnership, it is often less than that available in other business forms because a decision to bring in a new partner to raise needed money usually requires allocating some management responsibility to that partner. As noted below, limited partnerships, by contrast, can raise money from limited partners without conferring management responsibility as well.

## Advantages of Limited Partnerships

Another form of business is the limited partnership, which is a distinct legal entity created under state law. Every limited partnership has at least one general partner, who manages the limited partnership, and at least one limited partner. Limited partners have very little say in managing the business. In exchange for their limited control over partnership affairs, the limited partners have limited liability for partnership obligations: They are at risk only to the extent of their investment in the partnership. The general partner, by contrast, has unlimited liability for the partnership's debts and obligations. A limited partnership is formed by filing a certificate of limited partnership with the designated state agency, typically the secretary of state. The partners can structure their relationships with each other and address certain business issues through a limited partnership agreement.

### Pass-Through Tax Treatment

Although the tax treatment of limited partnerships is extremely complicated, if appropriate steps are taken, the income and losses of the business will, like those of proprietorships and general partnerships, flow through to the individual partners in accordance with their partnership shares. This structure avoids the double level of tax caused by a tax on the business itself.

### Financial Flexibility

Limited partnerships offer more financing opportunities than general partnerships because the former provide a vehicle for raising money (from limited partners) without having to take in the investors as general partners. In some instances, financing techniques are simpler to implement than those techniques available to corporations.

### Entrepreneurs in Action

John Smith wants to raise $100,000 to move his restaurant to a bigger and nicer location. John could create a limited partnership and offer investors limited partnership units at a cost of $25,000 per unit. In return for their investment, John promises the limited partners that he will pay back the $25,000 after five years plus give each limited partner 8 percent of the net profits of the restaurant during the five-year period. If John sells four units to different investors, he has his money and, as a general partner, he has retained his control of the business.

### *Limited Liability of Limited Partners*

In a limited partnership, a limited partner, whether a person or a business entity, is personally at risk for the obligations of the business only up to the amount invested in the partnership. The party's liability has been limited and personal assets cannot be used to satisfy the obligations of the business. In exchange for this limited liability protection, however, a limited partner is given a minimal voice in managing the partnership's affairs. A limited partner who participates in the management of the business in a more meaningful way will be stripped of this limited liability.

## Disadvantages of Limited Partnerships

### *General Partner Personally Liable for Business Debts*

Unlike limited partners, the general partner in a limited partnership is fully liable for the obligations of the business. In order to insulate themselves from unlimited personal liability for the debts and obligations of the business, many individuals who manage a limited partnership will establish a corporation, retain sole ownership of that corporation and have the corporation (which must be adequately capitalized) serve as the general partner. This machination may insulate an individual's personal assets from claims by creditors of the limited partnership, but it is expensive, cumbersome and adds additional layers of complexity to the business management process.

### *Limited Partners Lack Meaningful Management Responsibilities*

Another principal disadvantage of the limited partnership form is that it precludes a segment of its owners—each limited partner—from participating in the management of the business. Although most states provide some "safe harbor" rules specifying those management decisions that limited partners are free to participate in, unanticipated or ambiguous issues are bound to arise, and such rules offer little guidance. The penalty for a limited partner whose participation in management affairs exceeds designated limits? The limited partner loses its limited liability protection and has personal exposure for the obligations of the business. As a result of this draconian penalty, a limited partner may feel helpless watching the general partner make decision after decision that hurts the business and the limited partner's investment. The prospect of such helplessness often deters prospective investors from committing their capital to a limited partnership.

#### Entrepreneurs in Action

John Smith has been successful in selling two limited partnership units to friends and now has raised $50,000. He has approached several other friends who are all interested in investing with John but not without some say in management affairs. Because they would not be happy in the role of limited partners, they have advised John that they are not interested in the terms he has proposed. For the risk they would have to take as limited partners, they will invest only if John increases his rate of return from 8 percent to 18 percent. John is not happy but he is unsure how else to satisfy the potential investors and access necessary capital.

# Advantages of Corporations

The corporate form is now considered the leading business form in the United States. The industrial revolution required that entrepreneurs find a way for individuals to invest capital without risking their entire personal resources. Entrepreneurs also required a business form that would not require liquidating the business because one or more investors wanted to "cash in their chips." The corporation proved an almost perfect solution.

Regular (or C) corporations are formed upon the filing of a certificate of incorporation with the secretary of state or other designated official in the state where the business is to be established. Once established, corporations are recognized by law as distinct legal entities and have the power to act in their own name. Corporations are owned by shareholders, but managed by directors and, upon delegation of authority from directors, by officers as well. In many family or small businesses, individuals fill each of these different roles at the same time. Corporations provide their owners with a number of very attractive features, which are described below.

## Limited Liability for Business Owners

Corporations are treated by law as separate and distinct entities from their owners. As such, their liabilities are generally treated as separate and distinct from those of their shareholders. Consequently, shareholders of a corporation can generally feel secure that creditors of the corporation will not pursue them to satisfy claims. Also, shareholders are protected from claims by an individual sustaining personal injuries as a result of an action by an employee of the corporation or caused by one of the corporation's products.

### Entrepreneurs in Action

If John Smith sets up a corporation to own his restaurant, which he calls Smith Sandwiches, Inc., and a customer slips and breaks both legs, the customer will likely be limited to making claims for personal injury against the corporation. John's personal assets, including his $100,000 in the bank, remains safe.

## Piercing the Corporate Veil

Notwithstanding the generally recognized concept of limited liability, important exceptions have developed over the years that permit the "veil of protection" a corporation provides to its shareholders to be pierced so that the shareholders may be personally liable for certain corporate obligations. Although a detailed discussion of this doctrine is beyond the scope of this book, shareholders may be personally liable if

1. they have ignored the formalities required by corporate law, instead treating the business as their alter ego,
2. a shareholder's personal negligence caused personal injury, or
3. the corporation is insufficiently capitalized to carry out its operations and the shareholder(s) should have expected its undercapitalization to detrimentally affect a party doing business with the corporation.

Notwithstanding these exceptional circumstances, limited liability can, with careful planning, ordinarily be secured by shareholders of a corporation.

## The Continuity of Life

State law endows corporations with an indefinite and continuous life. This characteristic is attractive to an individual who, investing capital in a business, would not like the business wound up and dissolved on the unilateral decision by another investor to withdraw capital in the business or, alternatively, the death of a shareholder. While other business forms can be structured to achieve a measure of continuity, the corporate form does it best. Corporations such as General Motors, IBM and AT&T have survived long beyond the lives and business tenures of their initial shareholders and employees. The institutionalization of a corporation can provide significant competitive, financial and other advantages over businesses that lack such continuity.

## Transferability of Interests

A corporation is often desirable for owners who want a quick and cheap means to transfer their ownership interests in their business. When there is no agreement between shareholders to the contrary, shares of stock in a corporation are generally freely transferable. Indeed, shares of publicly owned corporations are routinely traded on stock exchanges through a phone call to a licensed broker. The convenience of transferability permits investors to move in and out of ownership positions in corporations with lightning speed if their investment philosophy or business circumstances change. By contrast, partners can generally not assign or transfer their interests in a partnership to another party without the consent of other partners. The high degree of liquidity is an important advantage of the corporation over other business forms, such as a partnership, where it may be difficult or impossible for a partner to conveniently retrieve money invested in the business.

## Management Flexibility

Corporations offer almost unlimited flexibility in structuring the management of a business as a result of the distinction made under corporate law between owners (shareholders), managers (directors) and day-to-day operators (officers). Augmenting this flexibility are the variety of tools available to customize the ownership and management responsibilities in a corporation. Common and preferred stock, preferred and subordinated debt, voting and nonvoting stock, high or low quorum requirements at directors meetings and veto rights for shareholders and/or directors are only a few of the many tools that owners of corporations can use to customize ownership and management rights and responsibilities.

# Disadvantages of Corporations (The Taxman Cometh)

Because corporations are treated as separate and distinct legal entities, they are also treated as separate and distinct taxpayers. Thus, the IRS and most state governments impose a tax on the income earned by a corporation, which must generally file its own tax return and pay its own tax based on its earnings. When the corporation distributes its income or assets to shareholders, another tax is imposed on the shareholders (either an income tax if the distribution takes the form of dividends or a capital gains tax if the distribution results from the sale or disposition of stock). As a result, income earned by a corporation is taxed twice. Despite limited exceptions where the double tax is not a material disadvantage to the shareholders of a corporation, such as the use of crafty income-splitting strategies (which are beyond the scope of this book), the second tax often raises the cost to business owners operating as a corporation.

# S Corporations to the Rescue

The Internal Revenue Code provides a limited solution to the double level of tax problem: It permits certain corporations to elect to be treated in accordance with the provisions of Subchapter S of the code. Unlike C corporations, "S corps" generally do not pay a corporate level tax on their earnings. Instead, all of an S corporation's earnings flow through to its shareholders who, like proprietors and partners, pay a single level of tax on the income of their business.

This pass-through tax treatment is an excellent solution to the double taxation problem and many small corporations have taken advantage of it. S corporations, however, are not for everyone. The IRS has established specific criteria that limit the eligibility of corporations to elect S status. These limitations are discussed below.

# Disadvantages of S Corporations

The most significant disadvantage associated with the S corporation form is that the IRS has limited its eligibility to corporations that meet the following four criteria:

1. The corporation must have no more than 35 shareholders.
2. All shareholders of the corporation must be U.S. citizens, resident individuals, estates or certain defined trusts (corporations, partnerships and many types of trusts *cannot* be shareholders).
3. The corporation may not have more than one class of stock.

4. The corporation may not have more than a 79 percent interest in any subsidiary corporations.

Any one of these limitations could easily present a problem to many businesses. Moreover, shareholders who initially meet the requirements for electing S status must continue to meet those requirements for as long as this status is desired. Even an inadvertent breach of the qualification rules can lead to termination of S corporation status. For example, if a new business is being capitalized by investors with different investment objectives, it might be desirable to issue two or more classes of stock (e.g., common stock and preferred stock). This decision would preclude S status. Similarly, a family-owned business that is founded by three siblings may elect S status at the commencement of operations but, after children, grandchildren and, perhaps, even great-grandchildren, the number of family member shareholders may easily exceed 35 and so require termination of S status.

### Entrepreneurs in Action

John Smith would like to expand the size and scope of his restaurant operations. In order to do so, he has decided he needs the help of a new owner. After considering a variety of individuals, he decides that his friend, George Newman, is the ideal candidate. George is energetic, talented and wealthy. They meet in John's lawyer's office to discuss combining their efforts. They are advised that, because George is a Canadian citizen and nonresident alien, they will be unable to elect S corporation status. For different reasons, the alternative business forms don't interest George and, ultimately, he decides to pass on the opportunity to work with John. John, of course, is very disappointed.

## Other Disadvantages of the Sub S Form

Aside from the difficulty of qualifying for S corporation status, the S election also can have adverse tax consequences notwithstanding its pass-through tax treatment. Some of these more important adverse consequences, including limits on the use of debt to create tax basis and the prohibition on the use of special allocation of corporate income, are considered in Chapter 8. Many other potential tax disadvantages of operating as an S corporation (which shareholders often learn of only upon audit by the IRS) are beyond the scope of this book.

## The Double Taxation Dance

One alternative for businesses that may not qualify for S corporation status yet seek the advantages of incorporation (limited liability, transferability of interests, management flexibility, etc.) is to do what I call the "double taxation dance." Let me explain its sometimes intricate steps.

As noted above, income earned by regular corporations is taxed twice, first, on the business entity level and, later, its shareholders are taxed again on the distributions they receive from the corporation. If, however, the corporation has no income, it pays no tax. Therefore, sophisticated entrepreneurs often operate their corporations in a manner designed to limit (not maximize!) income. Their maneuvering to limit corporate income, yet put as much money in their pocket as possible, can be so carefully orchestrated that it resembles a dance. For example, if the corporation can justifiably pay all of its income out in the form of tax-deductible compensation to its employees, the business has no income left to pay tax on. Another common means to limit (or even eliminate) corporate income is to finance the business with debt provided by shareholders. The corporation's payment of interest on the debt is also deductible and the repayment of the loan principal amount is tax free. This compares favorably with the distribution of equity to the same shareholders, which could be subject to a capital gains or ordinary income tax.

Other steps in this dance have been developed by creative attorneys and accountants seeking additional loopholes to avoid the double level of tax imposed on income earned by corporations. Many of these techniques (which, again, are beyond the scope of this book) are useful and may save shareholders thousands or, in larger corporations, millions of dollars. Nevertheless, there are limits to such creativity, and the IRS acts to close such loopholes by constantly developing and refining its arsenal of antiabuse restrictions. As a result, even with superb tax planning, most successful corporations ultimately pay a corporate-level income tax, which can be substantial. Many businesses grudgingly find themselves paying the additional tax as the price for the benefits of operating in corporate form. Other businesses, unwilling to pay the double tax price, elect not to operate in the corporate form and make due with the tools offered by other business forms.

## Analysis of Historical Business Forms—A Wrap Up

Before the enactment of legislation authorizing LLCs, business owners were faced with the choice of entity dilemma. Was it better to operate as a proprietorship, general partnership, limited partnership, S corporation or regular corporation? Each form offered advantages but each had disadvantages as well.

Proprietorships are easy to establish and the business income passes through to the proprietor, avoiding the double taxation attributable to C corporations. This business form, however, provides no flexibility in structuring ownership and no limited liability protection for the owner from the debts and obligations of the business.

Like proprietorships, general partnerships are easy to establish and have the benefit of pass-through taxation. In addition, a degree of ownership and management flexibility can be achieved by increasing or decreasing the ownership interests of the partners and by requiring a partnership agreement that spells out the basis for partnership relationships. Partnerships, however, have the same major disadvantage as proprietorships. The business owners—the partners—are personally liable for the obligations of the business.

Limited partnerships offer the advantage of pass-through taxation and, for the limited partners, limited liability protection. This business form, however, has a significant disadvantage: It precludes all limited partners from participating in the management of the business or risk losing their limited liability protection. A general partner in a limited partnership, moreover, has no automatic limited liability protection and may be forced to incorporate if that feature is desired.

C corporations offer limited liability protection for their owners (shareholders) and an extraordinary degree of ownership and management flexibility. Because, however, they are treated as separate and distinct legal entities, this business form incurs both tax on the corporate level and, again, on the shareholder level following a nondeductible distribution of income. This double level of tax can be extremely costly.

S corporations are, perhaps, the most attractive of the historical forms of business in most situations. This form offers the limited liability protection of C corporations but the pass-through tax treatment of a partnership. Also, like C corporations, S corporations, through use of the management tiers of shareholders, directors and officers, can offer significant management flexibility. However, S corporations have a substantial disadvantage: They offer very little ownership flexibility. Applicable Internal Revenue Code rules establish specific and important limitations on who can own an interest in an S corporation. Corporations, nonresident aliens, qualified retirement plans and most trusts are precluded from owning stock in S corporations. The 35-shareholder limit also can prove very restrictive. Other ownership limitations and its tax treatment of particular items are also significant disadvantages. In short, the S corporation can be a great vehicle for your business if you are able to qualify to use it.

## The Rationale for the LLC

A variety of forces, ranging from the impact of global competition, the need to attract foreign capital and the growing concern that U.S. businesses were being overtaxed, forced state governments to consider ways of improving their respective economic climates. Around 1977, Wyoming looked at the historically available forms of business and observed that foreign competitors had business forms that were superior to those available in that state. In other countries there were business forms that could provide the following:

- *Limited liability* (to protect its owners from becoming personally liable for the debts of the business)
- *Pass-through taxation* (to avoid the double taxation attributable to regular corporations)
- *No restrictions on permitted owners* (to eliminate the burdensome numerical and other requirements established for S corporations)
- *No restrictions on active participation* (to ensure that, unlike limited partnerships, all owners could be active in managing the business without jeopardizing their limited liability protection)
- *Operational flexibility* (to let owners structure the management in a way that satisfies the concerns and requirements for each business)

These business forms had many different names. In Germany, it was called a GmbH (Geselschaft mit beschrankt Haftung). In Latin America, it was called a Limitada; in France, a SARL. Canada had a similar form of business called a limited liability company. Wyoming decided to break ground in the United States and authorize the establishment of a similar form of business. It chose the name, which has since been chosen by 46 other states, *limited liability company* to refer to this new form of business in the United States. Let's explore the nature of LLCs and see why this business form, already so popular around the world, is now sweeping the United States.

# CHAPTER 2

# Bringing Your Business into the Future: An Introduction to Limited Liability Companies

Limited liability companies (LLCs) combine the flexibility and tax advantages of partnerships with the limited liability features of corporations. At the same time, they eliminate all restrictions on ownership, as well as legal restrictions on active participation by its owners, and they can be tailored to maximize the operational flexibility of the business. How attractive is this business form? Many lawyers and accountants now *presume* that every new business should be formed as an LLC. Let's examine why the LLC business form is getting such rave reviews and why it is such an important business tool for you to consider.

## What Is an LLC?

Like partnerships and corporations, an LLC is established and operated in accordance with laws enacted by state governments. Until very recently, LLCs were not authorized by most states. Lately, more and more states have enacted legislation that authorizes their use. LLCs can ordinarily be established to pursue the same lawful business purposes as proprietorships, partnerships and corporations. Restaurants, stores and car dealerships can all be LLCs. So can manufacturing, retail and service businesses. Even existing businesses can be converted to LLCs (see Chapter 9). In short, the LLC form is often suitable for the simplest family-owned operations as well as complex investment, real estate, joint venture and high tech businesses.

Because they were established to combine the best features of corporations and partnerships, the laws that create LLCs often read as if they had been written by state legislatures who cut and pasted their corporation and partnership laws together. For this reason, LLCs are often referred to as a hybrid business form. As a result, far from containing many new concepts and legal theories that would require a time-consuming learning process, you will find LLCs familiar and easy to work with. While the details of the LLC laws may vary by state, the basics remain generally the same. The owners of LLCs ("members") are protected by law from the personal obligations of the business in the same way that shareholders are protected from liability for the obligations of a corporation. In most other respects, including pass-through tax treatment, LLCs resemble partnerships.

It may also be possible for not-for-profit activities to be organized as LLCs, which could present tremendous opportunities for such organizations. Because not-for-profit ventures typically don't meet the narrow eligibility requirements for electing S corporation status, the only means they have to secure pass-through tax treatment has been to use a general partnership (with unlimited liability exposure) or a limited partnership (with unlimited liability exposure for a general partner or lack of control for a limited partner). LLCs may now provide an attractive opportunity for not-for-profits because they are able to provide limited liability protection, managerial control *and* pass-through tax treatment.

The opportunity to use LLCs for "nonbusiness" purposes could have important planning ramifications for individuals as well. For example, to secure the protection of limited liability, can an individual (who may feel uncomfortable with the extent of his or her insurance coverage) form an LLC to hold assets such as a personal residence, family automobiles and the like? If applicable, you should consider this opportunity with your advisers. Because of the possible unconventional use of an LLC in such circumstances, these potential uses should be considered in consultation with your attorney after review of your governing LLC act.

The recent explosion of LLC legislation has occurred at the state government level. There is no federal LLC legislation. Despite many similarities among most of the state LLC acts, each act is unique. Although a movement to adopt a uniform LLC law has begun, that day has not yet arrived.

### Planning Tip 2

LLCs have broad powers to conduct business, similar to those of corporations. Consider the merits of limiting your LLC's powers (or the power of its managers) by appropriate provisions in the articles of organization or operating agreement.

### Planning Tip 3

State legislatures or the federal government provide that specific types of businesses can only be operated in a designated business form. For example, banks, insurance companies and certain professional service companies are ordinarily required to operate as regular corporations. Although such restrictions are relatively limited, verify whether your type of business is eligible to operate as an LLC.

### Planning Tip 4

Because there is no uniform LLC law, the discussion that follows is necessarily general, and the law may vary in your jurisdiction. Therefore, be sure to consider the specific provisions of your applicable LLC law in structuring your business.

## Partnerships Versus Corporate Tax Classification

To understand how LLCs can obtain the most important benefit of the corporate form—limited liability—without its most important detriment—double-level taxation—we must consider how a business entity is classified for tax purposes by the folks at the IRS. Don't be alarmed: The following discussion is nontechnical. If you read it once (maybe twice) you will understand how LLCs are able to do all they do. We will also explore basic LLC terminology. When you're finished with this section, you will be well on your way to understanding how LLCs can work for you. Let's begin!

Federal income tax law recognizes only two types of entities through which two or more owners may conduct business, partnerships and corporations. Why? Because Congress never intended that the tax it extracts from corporations should be voluntary! It would make a mockery of the corporate tax system if businesses could secure all the desirable characteristics of corporations but, by calling themselves something else, could elect not to file corporate tax returns. Instead, Congress wisely decided that its tax on corporations should be imposed on businesses that are more like corporations than any other business. If an enterprise "walks and talks" likes a corporation, it must be a corporation and must pay a corporate tax.

Sounds simple, doesn't it? Until you pause and consider whether a particular business "closely resembles" a corporation. What does that mean? The United States Supreme Court was asked the same question, in 1935 to be precise, in a case called *Morrissey v. Commissioner.* In considering the proper classification of certain "express business trusts" that were used in that case to carry on a business, the Court stated that the test for "corporate resemblance" should be based on whether a particular business possesses the attributes that typify a corporation. The Court concluded that the particular trusts at issue in this case should be subject to a corporate-level tax because they possessed the five following corporate features:

1. Centralized management of the business
2. Limited liability of the owners
3. Free transferability of the ownership interests
4. Continuity of existence
5. The for-profit nature of the business

In 1960, the U.S. Treasury issued regulations designed to measure more precisely whether any particular business resembled a corporation for tax purposes. The Treasury Regulations incorporated the Supreme Court's analysis in the *Morrissey* case but sought to make the analysis even more objective to reduce the possibility of disputes on the proper characterization of a business. The 1960 Treasury Regulations distinguish partnerships from corporations by considering the presence or absence of the four following characteristics:

1. Limited liability
2. Continuity of life
3. Centralized management
4. Free transferability of ownership interests

The applicable Treasury regulations technically require consideration of two other characteristics as well: (1) the presence of business associates and (2) an objective to carry on a business for profit. Because, however, these two characteristics are common to both corporations and partnerships, they are ignored when characterizing a business for income tax purposes.

The regulations provide that a business shall be considered a corporation for income tax purposes if it has *more* corporate characteristics than noncorporate characteristics. Thus, if a business is found to have three or four of the foregoing characteristics, it will be characterized as a corporation and a corporate income tax will be imposed. A business with only one or two of these characteristics will be treated and taxed as a partnership, thus avoiding the corporate-level income tax. The IRS has previously concluded that each of the four factors should be given equal weight in the classification analysis.

On December 28, 1994, the IRS issued Rev. Proc. 95-10 (the Revenue Procedure) specifically relating to the tax classification of LLCs. The Revenue Procedure offers a set of guidelines to help ensure that an LLC secures favorable partnership tax treatment. Highlights of Rev. Proc. 95-10, which follows the tradition of the *Morrisey* case and the 1960 regulations, are considered below.

Since the treatment of an LLC as a partnership for federal income tax purposes is so important, and because many states permit LLC owners to select which of the relevant corporate characteristics they wish to use in their business, we need to consider the meaning of these four characteristics and the guidelines spelled out in the new Revenue Procedure. With a general understanding of them, you will better understand the structure of an LLC and how you can use your's to maximum advantage.

### Planning Tip 5

Although the classification of a business as a partnership or corporation is determined as a matter of federal law by application of the foregoing test, state law often determines whether the characteristics considered by this test are present or absent. For example, whether the restrictions imposed on an ownership interest placed in trust is a limitation on the free transferability of the interest may need to be answered by reference to the state's trust law. Accordingly, in determining the presence or absence of these factors in your business, consider the provisions of your state's applicable law.

### *Centralized Management*

*Centralized management* refers to a management structure where one or more, but less than all, owners of a business have exclusive authority to make decisions necessary to run the business. Corporations have centralized management, for example, because they are managed by a board of directors. General partnerships, on the other hand, lack this corporate characteristic because each partner has inherent power to act for—and legally bind—the partnership. LLCs may or may not have centralized management, depending on how they are structured. Without an agreement of the members to the contrary, all the members are charged with management responsibility, and the business will *lack* centralized management. The members of an LLC can also appoint one or more members or managers to manage the business. In that circumstance, the LLC may *have* centralized management. Because of its flexibility, many (perhaps an infinite) number of management structures in an LLC are possible. Determining whether a particular structure has or doesn't have centralized management can be a challenge. To help prevent inadvertently designing your management structure so that it possesses this corporate characteristic, states typically provide that, in the absence of an agreement to the contrary, an LLC is governed by all its members.

In its new Revenue Procedure, the IRS also gave some new guidance on centralized management in an LLC context. If members will manage their LLCs exclusively in their membership capacity, an LLC will lack centralized management. If members do not elect managers but do enter into internal agreements regarding decision making, centralized management should not be present. If the members are managing their LLC because they have all been designated managers under the terms of the operating agreement, it is unclear what result will be reached on the issue.

Other rules have been issued for LLCs that are managed by specially appointed managers. For example, if LLC members designate one or more members as managers, the IRS will ordinarily conclude that the LLC has centralized management unless the member-managers own at least 20 percent of the membership interests in the aggregate. Moreover, the IRS will not conclude that an LLC lacks centralized management if the member-managers must be periodically elected by all of the members or if the nonmanaging members have broad authority to remove the member-managers at their discretion.

### Planning Tip 6

Although the IRS has provided a number of helpful examples in its Revenue Procedure, it has acknowledged that it is not always easy to measure the presence or absence of this characteristic because of the many possible management structures. As a result, be prepared to advise the IRS of the facts and circumstances in your business that may help establish the (lack of) centralized management.

### Entrepreneurs in Action

If John Smith and Mike Harris are equal owners of a restaurant business, but Mike has entrusted the management responsibilities to John, the business clearly has centralized management. If, however, Mike and John both have management responsibilities, the business does *not* have centralized management. If John manages the business and can only be removed as a manager by Mike for particular and limited reasons (e.g., theft or dishonesty), centralized management likely exists. If Mike can remove John as manager for good reason, bad reason or even no particular reason, centralized management is unlikely to exist.

## Limited Liability

A business organization is considered to have the corporate characteristic of limited liability if, under local law, the owners are *not* personally liable for the debts and obligations of the business, including judgments, decrees and court orders. The liability is said to be limited (and not, for example, avoided) because an owner is still at risk of losing all or part of the money or other capital he or she has contributed to the business. Thus, for example, corporations are said to have limited liability because shareholders are not personally liable for the obligations of their corporation solely as a result of their ownership status. By contrast, general partnerships do not possess this characteristic because partners are personally liable for the obligations of the partnership.

LLCs, like corporations, provide limited liability to their owners. As a result, members or managers of an LLC are ordinarily not liable for any debts, obligations or liabilities of the business. This limitation applies regardless of whether the liability of the business is based on a breach of contract, personal injury or other cause. Claims by aggrieved parties must be brought against the LLC directly, not its members or managers. In the event a claim is asserted directly against a member, the member should be able to have the claim dismissed for having been improperly named as a defendant.

In many states, the members of an LLC can provide in their organizational documents that one or more members will be liable for some or all of the LLC's obligations or liabilities. Although use of this feature will likely be uncommon, it may be suitable for certain circumstances, such as when a lender is willing to extend financing only if at least one owner of the LLC is personally liable for the debt. Under the Revenue Procedure, the IRS will generally conclude that an LLC *lacks* the characteristic of limited liability if at least one member assumes personal liability for all of the LLC's obligations. The IRS has, however, established certain requirements that such a member must meet; for example, the member must have an aggregate net worth of at least 10 percent of the LLC's total contributions.

## Planning Tip 7

In a business with a substantial number of owners, centralized management and free transferability of ownership interest can be especially desirable. If this is true for your business, consider structuring your LLC to lack the characteristic of limited liability protection by providing that one member has unlimited liability for the LLC's debts and obligations. The member with unlimited liability may be a corporation. This planning option is complex and should be undertaken only upon advice of counsel.

## Planning Tip 8

Although there is still little precedent on the subject, courts can be expected to extend the doctrine of "piercing the corporate veil" (discussed in Chapter 1) to hold members of LLCs personally liable for conduct that would justify holding a shareholder personally liable in similar circumstances. Indeed, some states (including Colorado) have explicitly incorporated this concept into their LLC acts. Nevertheless, as in the case of corporations, your careful planning and attention to formalities should virtually eliminate the possibility that your LLC's "veil of protection" will be "pierced."

**Planning Tip 9**

Consider with your attorney what other related doctrines from corporate law might be "borrowed" for application to LLC jurisprudence. Consider, for example, the generally accepted corporate law principle of equitable subordination, which requires a corporation's shareholder who has a loan outstanding to the corporation to have the loan repaid only after all of the corporation's other creditors are repaid. The principle is generally applied only when the shareholder has acted in a manner that would make repayment of this loan before the other creditors unfair.

## Free Transferability of Ownership Interests

The Treasury Regulations provide that free transferability of an ownership interest in a business exists when an owner can fully substitute another person or entity in his or her place by assigning all of the owner's property rights—including both management rights and financial interests—in the business. An ownership interest in a corporation, for example, is considered freely transferable because a shareholder has the legal right (in the absence of an agreement to the contrary) to freely sell, gift, assign or otherwise dispose of his or her shares in the corporation to another. A partner's ownership interest in a partnership, by contrast, cannot generally be assigned without the consent of the other partners. Indeed, an agreement between partners permitting an unrestricted right to substitute another as a partner could result in a determination that the partnership has the corporate characteristic of free transferability for tax purposes. If an owner is able to freely transfer financial interests in a business (i.e., right to profits and losses) but *not* a governance interest, free transferability will not be deemed to exist.

To help ensure that LLCs will be taxed as partnerships, most state LLC acts provide that, in the absence of agreement by the members to the contrary, members can only freely assign their financial interests, but not their governance interests, in an LLC. In some states, this *default rule* cannot be modified. In other states, this rule can be modified by member agreement, but care should be exercised to avoid unwanted tax consequences. In its recent Revenue Procedure, the IRS gave additional guidance on this characteristic in the LLC context. In member-managed LLCs, if the consent of not less than a "majority" of the remaining members is required to transfer complete ownership interest, free transferability will be lacking. Majority may be defined as a majority in interest, a majority in capital or a majority determined on a per capita basis.

In a manager-managed LLC, if the operating agreement does not permit a member to transfer all attributes of the membership interest without the consent of at least a majority of the nontransferring member-managers, there is no free transferability. In either a member-managed or manager-managed LLC, if the transfer of a member's interest causes a dissolution, the characteristic of free transferability will be lacking.

### Planning Tip 10

Owners often agree that they can sell their ownership interests to a nonowner only if they have first offered their interests to other current owners, who choose not to buy them. Consider using this so-called right of first refusal when addressing the subject of free transferability in your LLC. If you preclude new owners from participating in the management of the business without the existing owners' consent, the interest is not freely transferable.

### Entrepreneurs in Action

If Mike Harris wishes to sell his ownership interest in the restaurant business to a close friend but needs John Smith's consent to do so, the IRS will not consider Mike's ownership interest to be freely transferable. This is true even if John cannot unreasonably withhold his consent to the transfer. By contrast, if Mike can sell his ownership interest in the business without John's consent, Mike's interest is freely transferable. Important conditions are sometimes attached to an owner's right to transfer interest. For example, if Mike is able to sell his shares to another *but* that person cannot participate in the management of the business without John's approval, the IRS will not consider Mike's interest to be freely transferable.

## Continuity of Life

The last of the four corporate characteristics, continuity of life, relates to whether a change in the ownership of a business will affect its existence. For example, corporations, which are deemed to be separate and discrete legal entities, have a potentially continuous and perpetual existence. They are not dissolved, terminated or otherwise discontinued simply as a result of a change in ownership. The Treasury Regulations provide that a business lacks continuity of life if the death, retirement, insanity, expulsion, resignation or bankruptcy of any owner causes the business to dissolve. In short, if a company dissolves or otherwise alters its identity by a change in the composition of the ownership, or certain changes in the owners' relationship to each other, the business *lacks* continuity of life. To help ensure that an LLC will lack this corporate characteristic, most state LLC acts provide that, without an agreement by members to the contrary, an LLC is automatically dissolved upon the death, retirement, insanity, expulsion, resignation or bankruptcy of any of its members. Members can use a wide assortment of factors to formally ensure that the business lacks continuity of life—even though, as a practical matter, continuity would virtually exist. For example, members of an LLC could provide that the business should only terminate upon the death of one designated member, say, the son of another member, who just turned one year old. To deal with the possible machinations, the IRS will again consider all of the facts and circumstances of an arrangement in order to determine the presence or absence of this factor.

In its new Revenue Procedure, the IRS, seeking to further clarify this analysis, ruled that a manager-managed LLC will generally lack continuity of life if (1) the members elect one or more managers and (2) the LLC's operating agreement provides that the death, insanity, bankruptcy, retirement, resignation or expulsion of each member-manager automatically causes a dissolution of the LLC unless it is continued by consent of at least a majority in interest of the remaining members. In member-managed LLCs, continuity of life is deemed to be lacking only if the dissolution event(s) apply to all members. Because the pool of member-managers is typically smaller than the pool of all members, linking an event of dissolution to member-managers only can usually contribute an additional degree of business stability.

As we shall see later, it may be possible to virtually secure the characteristic of continuity of life by having the owners agree (perhaps even in advance) that the business should continue following an event of dissolution. As long as meaningful events of dissolution exist, the characteristic of continuity of life should be deemed absent.

### Entrepreneurs in Action

If John Smith, sole owner of Smith Sandwiches, Inc., dies and leaves his stock in the corporation to his daughter, Jane, the company, for legal purposes, continues unchanged. If, by contrast, John had operated his business as a proprietorship, his business terminates upon his death. If appropriate provisions are made under John's will to transfer the assets of his proprietorship to Jane, she can establish a *new* restaurant business if she wishes. Because of this lack of continuity between ownership and the business, proprietorships lack the corporate feature of continuity of life. If John forms his restaurant as an LLC, he can generally choose whether or not to provide continuity of life. If he wants this characteristic, his LLC's articles of organization state that the business shall be continuous. If not, he specifies when it will terminate, either by reference to a particular date (a dissolution date) or to a particular event (an event of dissolution) such as the date he dies or retires as a member of the LLC.

**Planning Tip 11**

Consider with your attorney how to draft an operating agreement that minimizes the need for the remaining members' consent to continue the LLC after it has been dissolved.

## LLC Tax Classification

What does the tax treatment of partnerships and corporations have to do with LLCs? Practically everything! When Wyoming passed its LLC legislation, many experts were uncertain how LLCs would be treated by the IRS for income tax purposes. Would an LLC be taxed as a separate entity like a corporation or would its income pass through to its owners? The business world watched and waited. Little interest was shown by businesses or other states in adopting this new business form because of its uncertain tax treatment. Time passed and the Wyoming legislation came under careful scrutiny by the IRS. Finally, in 1988, the IRS determined that the Wyoming LLC it had been asked to consider had less than three corporate characteristics and, so, was properly taxable as a partnership for federal tax purposes. The IRS based its decision on the fact that Wyoming's LLC act provided (1) that a member could not assign the right to participate in the management of the LLC without the unanimous consent of the other members (i.e., there was no free transferability of ownership interests); and (2) the LLC would dissolve upon a member's dying or leaving the LLC unless the other members unanimously agreed to continue the business of the LLC (i.e., the business lacked continuity of life). In this case, the business had only the corporate characteristics of limited liability for its owners and centralized management. As a result, the IRS determined that the LLC was properly classified as a partnership for tax purposes.

The combined advantages of pass-through tax treatment, limited liability protection and management and operational flexibility that an LLC offers were immediately recognized by state legislatures following the IRS's favorable decision on the Wyoming LLC act. Between 1988 and February 1995, state after state passed new legislation authorizing the creation of LLCs. At this time, every state except Hawaii, Massachusetts and Vermont recognizes LLCs. State legislatures have addressed the importance of ensuring that LLCs formed under their acts would possess two or fewer corporate characteristics in two different ways. Some legislatures have enacted "bulletproof" LLC acts while others have enacted "flexible" LLC acts.

# "Bulletproof" LLC Acts

The term *bulletproof act* refers to a state law under which an LLC, formed in compliance with the very specific provisions and requirements of the law, automatically is taxed as a partnership for federal income tax purposes. This treatment is guaranteed because these laws are carefully designed so that an LLC can never have a majority (i.e., three or four) of the corporate characteristics discussed above. In other words, each bulletproof act is drafted to ensure that an LLC *lacks* at least two of the corporate characteristics. The tax treatment of an LLC formed under a bulletproof act cannot be challenged. There is no risk, no surprise, no guesswork. Because the essence of an LLC is to provide limited liability protection to its owners, these statutes all restrict an LLC's use of one or more of the other three corporate characteristics. Although a bulletproof LLC act lacks a degree of flexibility, it offers certainty of partnership tax treatment.

### Entrepreneurs in Action

John Smith and Mike Harris organize their restaurant business as a Wyoming LLC to ensure pass-through tax treatment. Because of the requirements of this state's LLC act, their new business will have the corporate characteristics of limited liability and centralized management. Their business, however, will lack continuity of life and the free transferability of ownership interests. John and Mike are pleased because not having free transferability means it will be unlikely one of them will sell his interest to another party who the other dislikes. As for lacking continuity of life, they decide that the business can always be continued following an event of dissolution if it makes sense to do so.

# Flexible LLC Acts

The term *flexible act* refers to a state LLC law that permits business owners the flexibility to fashion their LLC in a manner they find sensible for their situation. Flexibility has obvious advantages. A business owner who wants to secure centralized management and is unconcerned about continuity of life can form an LLC with the first corporate characteristic but not the second. Another business owner might want to set up a new business with the flexibility of an LLC but be taxable as a corporation in order to secure consolidated tax treatment. By tailoring the LLC to have a majority of corporate characteristics, the owner can achieve this result. These characteristics can, obviously, be combined in a variety of different ways. Such planning, however, would be impossible in a state with a bulletproof act.

A potentially serious consequence of tailor making your own LLC under a flexible act is that a misunderstanding about the significance of a provision or even a drafting error in your organizational documentation can cause a business to have a majority of corporate characteristics and, so, be unintentionally taxed as a corporation rather than a partnership. To help reduce this possibility, most flexible acts contain default provisions that automatically apply unless the members of an LLC agree to the contrary. Such default provisions help ensure the absence of corporate characteristics and the application of partnership tax treatment.

### Planning Tip 12

Carefully review your operating agreement to make sure that a drafting error does not cause your LLC to be unintentionally taxed as a corporation.

### Entrepreneurs in Action

John and Mike believe that limited liability and continuity of life are the two most important characteristics for their business. Instead of organizing their business under the Wyoming LLC act, they organize it under the laws of New York, one of the most flexible LLC jurisdictions. They prepare their organizational documents to provide these characteristics but not those of free transferability or centralized management. Because their business still has only two corporate characteristics, it should be taxed as a partnership.

# LLC Terminology

The terms used to describe the various players and their relationships with each other in an LLC are new but easy to understand. Because LLCs are a hybrid form of corporation and partnership, the new terminology closely resembles that used in these two other business forms. The terms discussed below are applicable to most LLCs but, because of the current lack of uniformity in state laws, it is possible that the terminology used in your state may vary slightly.

### *LLC*

Although we've already described the LLC business form, a simple definition is in order. An LLC is an unincorporated business, formed in accordance with procedures established by state law, that is eligible to be taxed as a partnership for federal income tax purposes. The owners of an LLC (members) are not personally responsible for the debts, obligations or other liabilities of the LLC. LLCs may sue and be sued as a distinct business entity. They also can hold legal title to property.

### Entrepreneurs in Action

Instead of establishing their business as a general or limited partnership or a regular or S corporation, John and Mike establish their business as an LLC. They agree to call it Smith Restaurants, LLC.

### Member

LLCs are owned by *members*. They are the equivalent of shareholders in a corporation or partners in a general partnership. Unlike S corporations which can have no more than 35 shareholders, an LLC is permitted an unlimited number of members. In some states, an LLC is only required to have one member although it currently remains unclear whether a one-member LLC can be considered a partnership for federal income tax purposes (since a partnership refers to a business with at least two co-owners). Because of this confusion, it is difficult to predict whether a one-member LLC will be taxed as a corporation, a sole proprietorship or, possibly, even as a partnership. In its recent Revenue Ruling, the IRS stated that it does not intend to rule on the proper classification of one-member LLCs, perhaps effectively shutting the door on this entity. In short, this is currently one of the more significant unanswered questions concerning the use of LLCs. My recommendation: Be safe. If possible, have at least two members in your LLC. As we will learn in Chapter 7, you may be better off with your spouse or children as co-owners of your business for estate planning reasons anyway, which is an easy way to avoid having to worry about this issue. If you do wish to be the sole owner, consider another business form. This is one of the few situations where it makes sense to do so.

### Planning Tip 13

At present, the following states explicitly require that an LLC have at least two members at all times: California, Connecticut, Delaware, Florida, Illinois, Iowa, Kansas, Maryland, New Hampshire, New Jersey, Ohio, Oklahoma, Oregon, Rhode Island, South Carolina, South Dakota, Tennessee, Virginia, West Virginia, Wisconsin and Wyoming.

States that explicitly permit one-member LLCs are Colorado, Missouri, New York and Texas. Nevertheless, federal tax treatment of one-member LLCs, as noted above, remains uncertain.

### Entrepreneurs in Action

Both John and Mike, as sole owners of Smith Restaurants, LLC, are technically known as members.

### Membership Interest

A member's ownership interest in an LLC is referred to as a *membership interest*. It is the equivalent of stock in a corporation or a partnership interest in a partnership. A membership interest confers on a member a right to a designated share of the profits and losses of an LLC, the right to vote and the right to receive distributions from the LLC. A membership interest is considered personal property so that members, like shareholders in a corporation and partners in a partnership, have no interest in particular property of the LLC. Membership interests can be conveniently reflected by the issuance of membership certificates.

### Entrepreneurs in Action

John and Mike agree that John's contributions to the business are more substantial than Mike's. As a result, they agree that John's membership interest entitles him to 60 percent of the profits, and Mike is entitled to receive the remaining 40 percent. They further agree to allocate any losses incurred by the business equally and that their voice in the management shall be equal as well.

## Articles of Organization

The *articles of organization* are analogous to the certificate of incorporation of a corporation and the certificate of limited partnership for a partnership. Articles are filed with the secretary of state or other designated official in the state where the LLC is established. Typical provisions in the articles are as follows:

- The name of the LLC
- The county where its principal place of business is to be located
- The date the LLC will be dissolved (if the business is not perpetual)
- An agent for service of process

Legislation may also specify other requirements, such as whether the LLC is managed by its members or by managers. Generally, LLCs are managed by their members, who vote in proportion to their ownership interests. If, however, the LLC is to be managed by one or more managers, the articles of organization should include a provision to that effect. Review the specifics of the law in the state in which you will be forming your LLC to make sure you are complying with all established requirements. See Appendix A for a sample form of articles of organization that John and Mike might use to establish their LLC. Chapter 12 includes a chart that sets forth:

- The title to each state's LLC act
- The title of the organizational document required to be filed (typically the articles of organization)
- The address and phone number of the office where such documents should be filed
- The fee that must be paid upon filing

### Operating Agreement

The *operating agreement* establishes the internal governance rules for the operation of the LLC business. Similar to the bylaws and shareholders' agreement of a corporation and the partnership agreement of a partnership, the operating agreement controls such matters as distributions of profits and losses, entry and expulsion of LLC members and how management powers are distributed among the members. Some states do not require operating agreements at all, and those that do require them do not always specify the form. As a result, the agreement can be detailed or brief, depending on the wishes of the members. If the members of an LLC decide not to have an operating agreement or to address only one or several subjects, the rules of operation set forth in the home state's LLC legislation will apply. In such a case, the LLC legislation operates by default. Thus, for example, if John Smith and Michael Harris form an LLC and do not otherwise provide in an operating agreement, they will each be entitled to an equal voice in the management as well as an equal share of the profits and losses of the business. (See Appendix A for a sample operating agreement between John and Mike.)

### Organizational Documents

The term *organizational documents* refers generically to either an LLC's articles of organization or its operating agreement, or both.

### Manager

All members of an LLC can manage the operation of the business, or the members can delegate such responsibilities to fewer than all of its members or to managers. A *manager,* who may be an individual, a partnership, a corporation or even another LLC, may, but need not be a member of the LLC. Managers may, but are generally not required to, appoint officers (such as a president, vice president, treasurer and so forth) to help run the LLC. Managers and officers are able to bind the LLC in accordance with the scope of authority conferred upon them by members. This may include the authority conferred under traditional rules of agency—such as apparent or implied authority. Accordingly, to help place innocent third parties on notice of the actual (as opposed to apparent) extent of their manager's authority, members of an LLC may wish to specify in their articles of organization the existence and scope, if any, of their manager's authority.

### Default Provision

If the members do not specify a particular aspect of their business relationship with each other in the operating agreement or the articles of organization, the rules in the appropriate state's LLC act apply by default. Provisions imposed on the members by operation of law, instead of by agreement between members, are known as *default provisions.* In some states, certain default provisions are deemed so important that they can't be changed even by agreement of the members. These are known as bulletproof provisions, or the acts known as bulletproof acts.

# Advantages and Disadvantages of LLCs

We began this chapter by noting that many professional advisers now presume that every new business should be formed as an LLC. Now that we've learned a little bit more about this new business form, lets consider just how well the LLC stacks up against the historical forms of business.

## *Comparison with General Partnerships*

Perhaps the single biggest advantage the LLC has over a general partnership is the limited liability protection it offers to its owners. As we learned in Chapter 1, a partner faces unlimited personal liability for claims against the partnership. By contrast, members have limited liability protection, which shields their personal assets from claims and obligations of the LLC business. Individuals with more than one business can form a separate LLC for each new venture and, so, not only protect their personal assets against business obligations, but also shield each LLC from the claims and obligations of the other LLCs.

Another advantage the LLC has over the partnership form is related to continuity of existence, one of the four corporate characteristics considered above. Under the Uniform Partnership Act, a partnership is automatically dissolved upon the death, withdrawal or other form of disassociation by a member. Although partners may agree to continue the business, a dissolution may result in such a circumstance. By contrast, an LLC can be structured to secure continuity of life or, like a partnership, the remaining members can always agree to continue the business in the same ways partners can following an event of dissolution.

As we will learn in Chapter 7, LLCs also offer advantages over general partnerships in estate planning opportunities. A parent, for example, could transfer all or part of an ownership interest in a business to a child while retaining exclusive management control of the business. Use of a general partnership to accomplish such objectives has a variety of disadvantages, including exposing the children (who may be inactive in the business) to personal liability claims for business debts and obligations. Also, the children, as partners, may have more decision-making influence than the parent would like. By contrast, an LLC affords the following advantages:

- Limited liability protection to both children and parents

- A well designed operating agreement to ensure that the business is managed by a capable party (for example, the parent-manager) even though the children own most or all of the business
- The possibility of multiple ownership classes to provide different forms of returns to different individuals—perhaps, for example, based on whether a child is active or inactive in the business

### Entrepreneurs in Action

Remember our patron who slips on a wet floor and breaks his legs in John's restaurant? If John and Mike had operated their business as a general partnership, there is no limit to their personal liability, and the injured patron could seek to recover from their personal (nonbusiness) assets in a lawsuit. If they operate as an LLC, their personal assets will be granted the same protection from parties making claims against the business that is available to shareholders of a corporation; their liability will be limited. Also, if Mike spends too much money and creditors bring suit because the LLC has failed to pay its bills, the creditors should only be able to seek payment from the assets of the LLC and not from John's or Mike's personal assets.

## Comparison with Limited Partnerships

LLCs also have an advantage over limited partnerships with respect to limited liability. As noted in Chapter 1, every limited partnership must have a general partner, who is liable for partnership obligations. Although a corporation can be formed to act as general partner, the need to establish such a corporation (which must be adequately capitalized!) adds to the expense and administrative inconvenience of owning and operating your business. LLCs dispense with such problems. All members have limited liability protection. Period.

In addition, limited partners may not participate in the active management of a limited partnership or they risk losing their limited liability protection. A limited partner who carelessly engages in what is later deemed to be active management of the business, may unintentionally lose his or her limited liability protection. By contrast, all members of an LLC are free to engage in the management of the business, subject only to compliance with the terms of their own operating agreement and articles of organization.

### Planning Tip 14

Ask your lawyer about the cost of establishing either a limited partnership or an LLC. The difference could be substantial. Consider the following comparison of the traditional organizational services your lawyer would render and bill for:

| *Limited Partnership* | *LLC* |
|---|---|
| 1. Prepares certificate of limited partnership. | 1. Prepares articles of organization. |
| 2. Prepares limited partnership agreement. | 2. Prepares operating agreement. |
| 3. Incorporates general partner. | |
| 4. Prepares bylaws for general partner. | |
| 5. Prepares shareholders' agreement for shareholders of general partner. | |
| 6. Completes S corporation election for general partner. | |

Although it's sometimes hard to tell with lawyers, two documents should be cheaper than six!

### Entrepreneurs in Action

When we last considered John doing business in the limited partnership form, he was having difficulty raising capital from potential limited partners who were concerned about the lack of opportunity to participate in the management of the business. If John forms his business as an LLC, he can provide these investors with any variety of managerial influence they may insist on. As we will learn later, different levels of management responsibility can be conferred on different investors. Unlike limited partners who lose their limited liability protection by becoming materially involved in management, these investors in an LLC will retain their limited liability protection no matter how involved they become in management affairs. In this case, the investors actually require relatively little management control but, in exchange for that right, John can keep his rate of return to the investors capped at 8 percent. He much prefers this tradeoff to having to pay investors 18 percent!

### Comparison with S Corporations

S corporations have received widespread attention and acclaim over the years by small business owners. The acclaim has been well deserved, since this business form combines pass-through tax treatment with limited liability. But the disadvantages associated with this form cannot be overlooked. S corporations must meet very strict and limited ownership qualifications. They can have no more than 35 shareholders, who must be either U.S. citizens or residents (a major drawback in an era of increasing global alliances), estates or certain types of trusts. An S corporation cannot be owned by a corporation nor may it own more than 79 percent of a subsidiary. This restriction limits the opportunity to create parent-subsidiary relationships. Finally, an S corporation cannot have more than one class of stock, which limits the opportunity to specify returns based on differing contributions to a business. If one of these eligibility requirements is breached, an S corporation can inadvertently lose its pass-through tax status.

All of these restrictions are inapplicable to LLCs! Foreigners, trusts of all types and corporations can all own membership interests in LLCs. LLCs cannot accidentally lose their pass-through status by a mere change in ownership. Also, LLCs can have an unlimited number of different membership classes. Members can be given an infinite variety of preferential or subordinated claims to such economic items as capital, profits, losses and cash flow (or some combination of the foregoing). Because of its inflexibility, S corporations must be careful when using debt-financing instruments because, if too many "equity type" interests are provided to the debtholder, the IRS can recharacterize the debt, treating it as equity. This result can destroy an S corporation's status because it would likely result in a second class of stock. By contrast, without any such limitations, financing an LLC with debt can be much more creative and flexible.

LLCs also have a number of tax advantages over S corporations, the basics of which are discussed in Chapter 8. For example, nonrecourse third party debt in an LLC can be used to increase the tax basis of its members. By contrast, such debt in an S corporation cannot increase a shareholder's basis. The bottom line? Potentially enhanced tax benefits available to LLC members that are not available to S corporation shareholders!

## Comparison with C Corporations

An LLC offers a number of significant advantages over C corporations. Most important is the double level of taxation on C corporations but not LLCs. Additionally, LLCs are not subject to the personal holding company tax, the accumulated earnings tax or even the alternative minimum tax (ATM). As discussed in Chapters 5 and 8, a member in an LLC can contribute services in exchange for a membership interest without tax problems while a shareholder can only do so by incurring a tax. These and other factors often make LLCs the clear favorite over C corporations.

Having considered some of the features of an LLC, you may conclude that the C corporation will be the first casualty of the historic forms of business. After all, who would ever want to pay the double level of tax? Not so fast! The C corporation form should be used in some instances. For example, owners of a business may find it desirable to have three or four of the corporate characteristics of limited liability, continuity of life, centralized management and free transferability of ownership interests. Depending on the flexibility of your LLC act, it may be impossible to secure each of these characteristics even with carefully drafted organizational documents. Second, federal tax and securities law requires that if a business publicly trades its ownership interest, it must be treated as a C corporation. Finally, C corporations permit certain tax-free employee benefits that are not permitted to partners in partnerships or members in LLCs. If a C corporation's taxable income can be completely eliminated by the payment of reasonable salaries, which are a deductible business expense to the corporation, this business form may be even more attractive.

### Planning Tip 15

Don't ignore the possibility that a C corporation can work for you. Consider your business strategy and objectives with your attorney before ruling out this option.

## Things To Consider before Using an LLC

By now, you should understand the excitement associated with LLCs shared by attorneys, accountants and other professionals who have studied this new business form. All the best features of the historic business forms rolled into one. Too good to be true? No. For a change, what appears to be a gigantic breakthrough really is.

Notwithstanding their significant advantages, LLCs do have certain limitations. Let's review some of the most significant of these drawbacks. You be the judge of their importance for your situation.

### Lack of Precedent

Because the LLC is a new form of business, little legal precedent is available to help owners predict how the law will be applied. Predictability is certainly a desirable feature for a business owner. Nevertheless, now that LLCs have been legalized in almost every state, this concern should quickly disappear. As more and more businesses are set up as LLCs, more and more issues will be clarified. Moreover, because LLCs are hybrid combinations of corporations and especially partnerships, it is likely that the established legal principles for these forms will quickly be extended by the legal system to LLCs as well.

## Lack of Uniform LLC Law

Currently no federal or uniform LLC act exists; each state LLC act is unique. As a result, there is some uncertainty how LLCs properly formed in one state will be treated in another state with a different LLC act or in a state that has not yet authorized the use of LLCs. Presumably the penalty in the latter scenario would be that such a state would not recognize the limited liability of an LLC's members if the business were operating within its jurisdiction. Perhaps. But, the significance of this concern needs to be reevaluated against the business climate in 1995. Currently, only Hawaii, Massachusetts and Vermont have yet to authorize LLCs. Every other state will presumably recognize LLCs formed in another state—and the limited liability protection available to their members. Although a lack of uniformity may create some problems for LLCs that operate in multiple states with varying legal provisions, most states provide that an LLC established in another state can "qualify" to do business in their state. Once duly qualified to do business, a foreign LLC should be treated essentially the same as a domestic LLC. For the typical small business that operates only in its home state, this issue is irrelevant.

## Lack of Standard Forms

Some observers have noted that because LLCs are so new, standard forms for such routine matters as opening bank accounts have not yet been adapted. In this era of computers and word processing, such a concern seems trivial at best and likely outdated by the time you read this.

## Federal Securities Limitation

Another apparent disadvantage of the LLC form is that it is available only to privately owned companies. If a company decides to go public, federal securities law requires that the business be operated as a C corporation. This problem, however, seems manageable. It is relatively easy for an LLC to switch to a C corporation if the business goes public. A new corporation would be formed and the assets of the LLC transferred to it. Not too hard. In any event, the same federal securities law requires similar treatment for general and limited partnerships as well as for S corporations. Any business operating in one of these other forms would also need to convert to a C corporation in the event it goes public.

## Loss of Pass-Through Tax Treatment

In states with flexible LLC acts, members can vary the structure of their LLC with respect to transferability of ownership interests, continuity of existence, centralized management and limited liability. Although this opportunity often makes the flexible LLC legislation preferable to the alternative, bulletproof legislation, the potential for problems is apparent. If members inadvertently structure their LLC in a flexible LLC state so that the business has three or four corporate characteristics, the business will be taxed as a corporation, not as a partnership. The loss of favorable pass-through tax treatment may be unexpected and unwanted. Supporters of LLCs correctly observe that this problem is not with the business form but with the user of the form. The easy solution is to seek competent professional advice in structuring your LLC or, as any good business owner would do, pay close attention to the statutory requirements. You can avoid this problem with a modicum of care.

### Desire To Secure Corporate Characteristics

Certain businesses may prefer having a majority of corporate characteristics. For example, a business with many owners may require or prefer limited liability, centralized management and free transferability of ownership interests (because of the unwieldy number of remaining members who would have to approve the transfer). Such businesses could, potentially, choose between operating as a corporation or, in flexible LLC act states, an LLC that is treated for tax purposes as a corporation. Use of an LLC in such situations may have desirable long-term tax and other benefits.

### State Tax Treatment

Some states impose income or franchise taxes on LLCs or require LLCs to pay certain annual fees while not imposing like taxes or fees on partnerships or S corporations. For example, in New York state, LLCs must pay an annual filing fee of $50 per member, with a minimum fee of $325 and a maximum fee of $10,000. An identical business that has been formed as a partnership will not incur such a fee. Although the expense resulting from use of an LLC usually pales in comparison to the advantages conferred on the owners, a careful analysis of such expenses should not be ignored. Accordingly, consider the tax treatment of LLCs in the state where your business will operate.

### One-Member LLCs

Finally, if the business must have only one owner, the LLC, at this time, is probably a poor choice. Although the subject of one-member LLCs continues to be debated, and some states even expressly authorize their use, the risk exists that such businesses could be taxed as corporations (double-level tax!). This conclusion is based on the commonsense observation that in order for a business to be taxed as a partnership, there must be at least two partners. Although case law may develop, and one-member LLCs may become commonplace, I suggest that, unless you're a gambler, you consider letting others establish this precedent for you.

Disadvantages? Judge for yourself in consultation with your advisers. If you compare the advantages and disadvantages of an LLC to those of every other business form, you may find that you too can profit by forming your own LLC!

# CHAPTER 3

# How To Form Your Limited Liability Company

Now that you've considered the available options, you're convinced that you should establish your business as an LLC. What do you do? How do you begin? Where do you establish your LLC? Relax. Catch your breath. This may even be a good time to take a break. When you're ready to continue, this chapter will answer your questions and show you how you can form your own LLC.

## Begin by Selecting the State of Organization

The first decision you must make in forming your LLC is choosing which state's law to use. Do you form your LLC in your home state or another state? If you decide to use another state, which one? Traditionally, Delaware has been a popular state for business owners forming corporations because it offers extensive precedent, a business-oriented judicial system and cutting edge legal policy set by its state legislators. Does Delaware continue to make sense when setting up an LLC?

Although no easy answers are available, there are some sound principles to consider with your advisers. First, for a typical small business, the two obvious benefits to using your home state's LLC law are a degree of convenience and a likelihood that your advisers will be more familiar with the law and practice in their home state than in another state.

If you live in a state with a bulletproof LLC law, you need to decide whether you value the certainty of partnership tax treatment that law provides or whether you would prefer to tailor your LLC using the provisions of another state's flexible LLC law.

If particular legal principles are important to you, consider selecting a state that has explicitly adopted such principles. For example, if you are concerned about your rights as a minority owner of an LLC in the event of a dispute with the majority owner, verify that your home state's law offers ample protection to minority members. If not, you may want to utilize another state's law that offers appropriate protection. If you want to form a one-member LLC but your state doesn't permit its use, you may be able to form your LLC in a state that does permit one-member LLCs and then qualify the LLC to do business in the state where it will do business.

Finally, for the time being, if you're a business owner in Hawaii, Massachusetts or Vermont and you want to establish an LLC, you have no choice but to form your business under another state's law. You should discuss with your advisers, however, how the business would be treated in your home state.

### Planning Tip 16

When choosing which state to organize your LLC in, consider your business and personal objectives. Because state LLC laws vary, you may accomplish your objectives more easily by forming your LLC in a strategically selected state.

## Select an Organizer

An organizer is responsible for establishing the LLC in accordance with applicable state law requirements. An organizer, who fills a role similar to that of an incorporator of a corporation, forms an LLC by filing articles of organization with the appropriate secretary of state or other designated state official. Most state LLC laws allow any individual or other business entity, including a corporation or even another LLC, to be not only members of an LLC but also an organizer. Organizers are generally not required to be members of LLCs. Some of the earliest state LLC acts require that two or more organizers are required to file articles of organization; the trend in more recent state acts is to permit a single organizer to form an LLC.

### Planning Tip 17

Use the flexibility permitted in organizing an LLC to expedite the formation process and, if appropriate, maintain confidentiality by having a nonmember (perhaps your attorney) form the business.

# Consider the Merits of a Pre-Formation Agreement

Because establishing a business with two or more members can be complex and filled with potential for misunderstandings, it may be prudent to document certain agreements between prospective members before the actual formation of a new LLC. Such a document, which is sometimes called a *pre-formation agreement,* should be signed by all the prospective members of an LLC and should contain all the material terms of their deal with each other, including the manner in which their internal affairs will be governed. A pre-formation agreement could be useful for an individual organizing a new LLC to document the disclosure of relevant information to new members, including potential risks associated with an investment in the LLC. Such disclosure may help reduce later claims by a dissatisfied member that he or she was wrongfully or fraudulently induced to purchase an LLC membership interest on the basis of overoptimistic information.

### Planning Tip 18

Consider using a pre-formation agreement to cover many or even all of the subjects that will later be included in the LLC's operating agreement; it can help reduce the time and expense of preparing the operating agreement, when necessary.

# Prepare Articles of Organization

An LLC is formed by the organizer filing articles of organization with the appropriate secretary of state or other designated state official, the same state agency that is responsible for overseeing the filing of a corporation's articles of incorporation and a limited partnership's certificate of limited partnership. The business is ordinarily effective on the filing date or, if permitted by state law, a later date specified in the articles of organization. The state official will then provide the LLC with a certificate of organization that is conclusive evidence of the LLC's proper formation. As discussed below, some states require the articles of organization or a summary of them to be published in specified newspapers. Until this requirement is met in such states, an LLC may not be considered formed or, alternatively, capable of instituting a legal action. Although you need to verify the particular filing requirements under the state law you ultimately decide to use, the required contents of the articles are generally minimal. They include the following:

- The name of the LLC
- The county within the state where the LLC's office will be located
- A designation of an agent (e.g., secretary of state) for service of process

- A statement about whether the LLC is to be managed by its members or by one or more managers
- If applicable, a statement that one or more of the members may be liable for specified debts or obligations of the LLC
- A statement specifying the duration of the LLC (i.e., the date the LLC is to be dissolved if it lacks continuity of life)

Verify whether your state has additional requirements. For example, Florida requires a brief statement of the terms and conditions upon which new members can be admitted and a statement of the total cash and property the members have initially contributed to the business. Minnesota requires an LLC's articles of organization to state whether the members have the power to enter into a business continuation agreement in the event of a member's disassociation. Exercise care in preparing these articles, since poor drafting can have unexpected tax consequences. For example, if your LLC is structured to have a limited duration (and, so, lack the corporate characteristic of continuity of life), the articles should state a time or event upon which the LLC shall dissolve, and the operating agreement should contain a similar or identical provision to ensure that the members have the power to dissolve the LLC. Notwithstanding the potential traps for the unwary, LLCs are easy to set up properly. Let's examine a standard form of articles of organization so you'll see just how easy it is. For your ease of reference, a sample form of articles of organization is set forth in Appendix A.

### Naming Your LLC

Virtually all state laws require that an LLC be identified as such in its name. As a result, these statutes generally require the name of the business (which must be distinct enough so it won't be confused with another business) to be followed by one of the following or similar designations:

- limited liability company
- LLC
- LC
- Ltd.

Once an LLC has filed its articles of organization in its home state, or qualified to do business in a foreign state, no other business can use the exact same name in those states.

### Entrepreneurs in Action

John Smith and Mike Harris decide to call their LLC Smith Restaurants, LLC. Once they have filed their articles of organization with the New York secretary of state, they are assured of the exclusive right to use this name in New York. Unless they also properly qualify to do business in every other state, other businesses can secure the exclusive right to use this name in other states.

### Planning Tip 19

All or most state LLC acts provide that a particular name can be reserved or saved before the actual establishment of the business. Use this feature if you need to protect your name but your business is not quite ready to begin operations. Most states provide that a name can only be reserved for a specified period (e.g., 60 days). Although extensions can often be secured, the reservation process cannot be used to save a name in perpetuity. A sample application to reserve a name form is shown in Appendix A.

## *Establishing Your LLC Office*

LLC laws throughout the United States require that articles of organization identify the county within the state where the LLC's office will be located. A majority of state LLC laws permit the use of an address even if the LLC does not conduct business there. No telephones. No employees. Technically, not even a mail drop. The address fulfills the requirement that the LLC has a presence in the state in order to be established under state law. A small minority of states do, however, require that the LLC maintain a physical office in their state to satisfy this requirement. Check this point with your advisers.

## *Designating an Agent for Service of Process*

LLC laws also uniformly permit LLCs to both bring lawsuits in their own right and also to be sued. This feature derives from the premise that LLCs, like corporations, are distinct legal entities and not simply a collection of individual members. To make sure that LLCs cannot avoid the responsibility of defending their conduct in a lawsuit by concealing their location and avoiding service of process, state law requires that an agent be designated in the articles of organization. The LLC's designation authorizes the agent to accept service of process and similar legal notices on its behalf. The agent, in turn, is obligated to forward such notices to the LLC's last known address. Make sure that designated agents meet applicable state law requirements and, if you make a change in agent, that appropriate steps are taken to reflect the change. State corporation laws contain a similar requirement.

## Management by Members or Managers

State LLC laws permit LLCs to be managed by members or managers. Unless the articles of organization specifically delegate management responsibility to one or more managers, every member is, by default, responsible for the management of the LLC. In a member-managed LLC, every member acts as an agent of the LLC and is generally able to bind the LLC. An LLC's operating agreement may limit the member's authority, although such a limitation may not be effective unless the person who seeks to enforce the member-created obligation against the LLC was aware of that member's limited authority at the time the obligation was created.

The members of an LLC may delegate any or all management responsibilities to one or more managers, who may or may not also be members. Most states permit individuals or legal entities, including corporations or other LLCs, to serve as managers. Members can even establish different classes of managers so that different managers can be made responsible for different roles. Although the rules in this area are complex, it is safe to conclude that if an LLC is managed by all of its members it will lack the corporate characteristic of centralized management. A business that elects one or more managers will generally possess this characteristic.

### Planning Tip 20

As discussed in Chapter 2, be careful that your business has two or fewer corporate characteristics to secure partnership tax treatment.

### Planning Tip 21

If the members prefer that your LLC be managed by managers, include a specific provision to that effect in the articles of organization. Because of its importance, the subject of management is treated in more detail in Chapter 4.

## Member Liability for Specified Debts

LLCs are typically formed to secure limited liability for its members. Accordingly, this corporate characteristic is nearly always present in LLCs. There may, however, be sound reasons to provide for the general liability of one or more LLC members in narrow instances. For example, if a business prefers to be taxed as a partnership, but it values the corporate characteristics of free transferability of interests and centralized management more than limited liability, this last feature could be eliminated. If one or more members are to be personally liable for all or specified debts of the LLC, the articles of organization should include a statement of such liability.

### Planning Tip 22

When using this planning opportunity, consider whether the member with general liability for an LLC's debts and obligations should be a corporation. This structure is sometimes preferable to that of a limited partnership using a corporation as a general partner because the members of the LLC, unlike the limited partners, remain free to participate in the management of the business without risking exposure to its liabilities.

## The Duration of the LLC

In order not to have a majority of corporate characteristics, LLCs generally do not have continuous and perpetual existence. If not otherwise required by state law, members of an LLC secure this result by providing in their articles of organization that their business shall be dissolved when a particular event occurs. Common provisions ensuring dissolution include the following:

- Establishing a date in the articles of organization for the dissolution to occur
- Specifying that a sufficient percentage of members can consent to a dissolution
- Establishing particular events, such as the death or bankruptcy of a member, as a grounds for dissolution.

In many LLC acts, default provisions stipulate that an LLC will be dissolved upon the bankruptcy, death, dissolution, expulsion, incapacity or withdrawal of any member. These provisions also help ensure that an LLC lacks the corporate characteristic of continuity of existence and, as a result, is taxed as a partnership.

### Planning Tip 23

In a flexible LLC jurisdiction, you may be able to vary default dissolution provisions by member consent. If you do so, be careful that you don't inadvertently confer perpetual existence on your LLC!

### Planning Tip 24

To minimize the potential adverse consequences of dissolving an LLC simply because a trigger event occurs, consider (with your adviser) providing in your operating agreement that the business shall be continued upon the unanimous or majority consent of the remaining members. This subject is addressed in Chapter 10.

## Pay Any Filing Fees

Most states impose filing fees in connection with establishing and, later, maintaining an LLC. Such fees are typically paid upon the filing of certain organizational documents such as the articles of organization, certificates of merger and certificates to terminate existence. These fees are typically nominal but their importance is clear. A failure to pay required filing fee payments will prevent your LLC from being formed or, after formation, could cause a forced dissolution of the business. An information chart appears in Chapter 12, which, among other things, shows the current fees required upon formation of an LLC.

## Fulfill Any Publication Requirement

Many states require either a copy of the articles of organization or a summary of its substance to be published in a local newspaper on one or several occasions. In such states, proof of publication must be filed with the secretary of state or other designated official. The typical consequence of failure to comply with publication requirements is that the LLC will be precluded from bringing any legal action to enforce its rights against another party. Theoretically, an LLC could delay complying with this requirement until it needs to bring a lawsuit, but such a sloppy practice should not be encouraged. The requirement is minimal and can be readily satisfied with little hassle or expense. Just do it!

## Prepare an Operating Agreement

LLC acts authorize the members of a business to enter into an operating agreement. Sound strange? It's not. Think of it as the equivalent of a partnership agreement or a shareholders' agreement, which is never required by law but is usually an important document. An operating agreement provides a legal mechanism by which LLC members can structure their internal relationships and affairs. Through this document, you can tailor your relationship with your fellow owners. Operating agreements typically set forth the understanding reached by members on required capital contributions, distribution of profits and losses, admittance of new members, restrictions on the transfer of a member's interest in the LLC and a host of related matters. If a subject is not otherwise addressed in an operating agreement, the rules set forth in the appropriate state's LLC act will apply by default. Because of the virtually limitless subject matters that could be important to an LLC's members, an LLC act may be silent on how the subject should be treated. If a substantial dispute on the subject arises between members, you may find yourself at the mercy of a judge who can only guess what the proper arrangement should be. Therefore, if a subject is important to your LLC, be sure to address it properly in your operating agreement. Because a good operating agreement is so important, consider the following preliminary suggestions for yours.

## Put Your Agreement in Writing!

Because an operating agreement governs the internal affairs of an LLC, it is ineffective unless it is unanimously approved by all of the members. Although some states such as New York require that an operating agreement be in writing, a number of other states permit the use of oral operating agreements. Don't be tempted to take the easy way out. Put your agreement in writing, even if the law does not require it. Putting your agreement in writing will help ensure that you and the other members carefully think through the often complex issues of how your relationship should be ordered. More important, in the event of a dispute, a written agreement is always preferable to an oral one in helping resolve what the members actually agreed to.

## Specify How To Amend Your Agreement!

As you know, change is inevitable and, as often as not, unpredictable. Customers are won and lost, new products and markets are developed and old ones discarded, members retire, lose interest or die. Although you can do nothing to prevent change, you can anticipate it. Consider how these and other factors might affect your LLC. Would your current operating agreement serve its purpose well in such circumstances? Unless the operating agreement or articles of incorporation provide otherwise, the operating agreement can only be amended with the *written* consent of *all* members whose obligations, tax status or distributions would be adversely affected by an amendment. If you think a less onerous amendment process should be followed, consider including it in your initial operating agreement.

## Review Your Agreement with an Attorney!

Unlike articles of organization, which must be duly prepared and filed for an LLC to be established, an operating agreement need never be prepared and, if prepared, typically need not be filed with the designated state office. The legal consequence of not entering into an operating agreement, or of entering into an unenforceable agreement, is that the provisions established under your state's LLC law apply by default. Because, however, one of the LLC's significant advantages over other business forms is its flexibility in ordering the relationships among members, entering into an operating agreement is typically desirable. This flexibility can quickly turn an operating agreement into not only a very complex legal agreement, but one that can significantly affect your tax status as well. For example, in states with flexible LLC acts, even a simple drafting error can inadvertently bestow an additional corporate characteristic on your LLC, causing it to be taxed as a corporation. In recognition of the complexity and opportunity for mishap, consider retaining an attorney familiar with LLCs to draft your operating agreement or, at a minimum, let an attorney review the agreement you've prepared.

## Suggested Contents for Your Operating Agreement

Assuming you are permitted the flexibility to do so by your state's LLC act, consider, at a minimum, addressing the following subjects in your operating agreement:

- Management by member or manager
- Capital contribution obligations
- Allocations of profits and losses
- Transferability of membership interests
- Consequences of disassociation by a member
- Admission of new members
- Trade secrets and confidential information
- Dispute resolution
- Fiduciary duties members owe to each other
- Partnership tax treatment matters
- Duration of LLC
- Dissolution events
- Winding up and termination

Because of their importance, each of these subjects is separately discussed below in more detail.

### Planning Tip 25

Prepare a thorough and well-drafted operating agreement that may also address the following subjects:

- Voting procedures a id quorum requirements
- Member access to records
- Buy-sell provisions
- Duties of members (and managers, if applicable)
- Provisions for meetings

Remember that LLCs are, in many instances, like other businesses and the traditional provisions found in partnership and shareholder agreements, bylaws and similar documents merit inclusion in your LLC operating agreements as well.

### Planning Tip 26

An LLC's articles of organization document is a public record that must be filed with an appropriate state official. By contrast, an operating agreement is not required to be filed and thus need not be a matter of public record. If you have the option to include a provision in either your LLC's articles of organization or its operating agreement, using the latter vehicle will help keep your company's affairs confidential.

### Planning Tip 27

The provisions of an operating agreement are generally ineffective with respect to third parties if they have been kept confidential as between owners. Thus, you may wish to give special notice to appropriate third parties about specific provisions in your operating agreement to ensure that they are bound by the terms of the agreement.

### Entrepreneurs in Action

John and Mike include a provision in their operating agreement that neither one of them can enter into a contract in excess of $10,000 without the consent of the other. Accordingly, when they decide that Mike should negotiate with a landlord to rent space at a cost of $50,000 per year, John may wish to send a letter to the landlord advising that both Mike and John's consent is necessary to approve a lease agreement.

## Management by Member or Manager

As previously noted, LLCs can be managed by a class of members, or one or more (e.g., three) or classes of managers (e.g., managers of operations, managers of finance, etc.). Although an LLC's articles of organization should state which management structure will be used, the operating agreement can address management issues in more detail. Because of the significance of management issues, this subject is considered in more detail in Chapter 4.

## Capital Contribution Obligations

LLCs acts generally recognize that various ways of contributing capital for a business are sufficient for acquiring a membership interest. For example, many states provide that a member may contribute capital to an LLC in the form of cash, property, services or a promise (often required to be in writing) to make a future contribution of cash, property or services.

Like a shareholder's capital contribution to a corporation, a member's capital contribution to an LLC represents an equity investment in the business that the member is at risk of losing if the business is unable to meet its obligations. This risk of loss to a member who makes a *present* capital contribution in exchange for a membership interest is clear. In addition, a member who receives a membership interest today in exchange for a promise to make a *future* capital contribution is at risk because the member's promise is a contractual obligation. The LLC or its creditors can seek to compel payment of a delinquent contribution against the member or his or her estate. Basic financing considerations and tax consequences are discussed in more detail in Chapters 5 and 8. A good operating agreement spells out such fundamental matters as which member will contribute what capital; how additional capital should be raised in the future, if necessary; and how noncash contributions will be valued and recorded. Failure to reach agreement on such critical issues is a prescription for the failure of your business!

### Planning Tip 28

Corporations are ordinarily prohibited from issuing stock to a prospective shareholder in exchange for a promise to make a future contribution of cash, property or services. Use the flexibility of LLCs to recognize various ways that capital can be contributed in exchange for membership interests, including promises to make future contributions, to your advantage.

### Planning Tip 29

Don't be misled into thinking that a promise to make a capital contribution to an LLC in the future is risk free. Your failure to make such a contribution can be grounds for legal action against you.

### Planning Tip 30

Consider specifying in your operating agreement the consequences of a member's failure to make a required capital contribution. Requiring payment can sometimes be onerous, impossible or, in the case of a spouse of a deceased member, even unfair. Instead, an operating agreement can provide that a member's failure to make a promised capital contribution shall result in one or a combination of the following consequences:

1. Reduction of a member's interest
2. Complete elimination of a member's interest
3. Forced sale of a member's interest at agreed upon terms

4. Subordinating the defaulting member's interest to that of the nondefaulting member's interest
5. Requiring the defaulting member to contribute cash in lieu of the property or services that cannot be contributed

### Entrepreneurs in Action

Mike Harris promises John Smith that, in exchange for a 50 percent membership interest in Smith Restaurants, LLC, Mike will provide construction services to build a new restaurant next year. The value of this service is agreed to be $300,000. Mike and John could provide in their operating agreement that if, for any reason, Mike is unable to provide these services, he must pay $200,000 in cash and his interest will be reduced from 50 percent to 40 percent. The members could even agree that different reasons for the failure may have differing consequences. For example, Mike may be unable to provide construction services because his workforce is on a strike or, alternatively, he is unable to secure necessary bank financing because he has overleveraged himself on unrelated projects. John may feel that the consequences to Mike for a failure to contribute capital as a result of the first circumstance should be different from those of the second circumstance. Your operating agreement can be used to identify a variety of consequences for varying causes of a member's failure to contribute capital as required.

## *Allocation of Profits and Losses*

All state LLC acts specify how, without an agreement to the contrary, the profits and losses of the LLC should be allocated to its members. The two most common forms are to allocate profits and losses equally among members and to allocate them on the basis of each member's unreturned capital contributions. Either of these default provisions may not fairly reflect the members' expectations or the economic reality of their respective contributions. Subject only to applicable tax rules discussed below, an operating agreement can specify any other basis upon which profits and losses should be allocated.

In the absence of an agreement, most LLC acts provide that distributions can only be made in cash. If distributions of property are permitted, LLC acts generally require that no member can be forced to accept more than his or her pro-rata share of such property, and other members are required to accept their pro rata shares. An operating agreement can specifically authorize noncash distributions, such as equipment, land or patents, as well as to specify that some, but not all, members can be compelled to accept more or less than a pro-rata share of such noncash distributions.

### Entrepreneurs in Action

John Smith agrees to provide $50,000 cash for working capital and Mike Harris agrees to supply agreed-upon inventory (food supplies) that are projected to cost $50,000 for their LLC. If, because of floods, drought or other natural disaster, Mike actually spends $100,000 for these supplies, he will have contributed more than John. To avoid an unfair result, the members could provide in their operating agreement that the first $50,000 of profits from their business should be allocated to Mike to prevent unfairness.

### Planning Tip 31

Consider using your operating agreement to establish how your LLC will make distributions.

### Planning Tip 32

Consider specifying in your operating agreement how noncash distributions will be made to enhance management and operational flexibility.

### Planning Tip 33

As discussed in Chapter 5, an LLC cannot make a distribution to members if, after the distribution, the LLC's liabilities exceed the fair market value of its assets. Avoid making or receiving a distribution in violation of this provision. Violators may be required to refund the value of the distribution to the LLC.

### Planning Tip 34

Consider including a provision in your operating agreement, subject to legal standards, mandating that distributions be made periodically (and at least once a year) so that members can pay their taxes on their allocable share of LLC income.

## Transferability of Membership Interest

LLC membership interests are generally considered to be personal property, just like stock in a corporation or a partnership interest. Like other types of personal property interests and in the absence of an agreement to the contrary, a membership interest in an LLC can be sold, assigned or given away to another. The default provisions of some state laws specify that a new member can acquire all of a prior member's rights and interests (e.g., financial and management) only upon the unanimous or majority consent of other members. These default provisions help ensure the absence of the corporate characteristic of free transferability. LLC members may impose additional restrictions on transferability or eliminate having such restrictions altogether. The members' wishes can be secured through appropriate provision in an LLC's operating agreement.

Among other things, members can agree whether financial interests only can be freely transferred or governance and management rights as well. A well-drafted operating agreement also will establish procedures for approving of such transfers by the continuing members. In drafting suitable language for your business, consider whether provisions in your LLC act place conditions or limitations on this subject. For example, Texas provides that a member can only transfer the financial component of his or her membership interest without limitation; the right to participate in the governance or management of the LLC requires the consent of the other members. As a result, a new member in a Texas LLC is only able to share in the profits and losses that had previously been allocated to the prior member unless the other members consent to the transfer of the governance interest as well.

Also, be sure to consider whether your chosen restrictions will be respected by the IRS. For example, in a recent Letter Ruling, the IRS considered a restriction on transferability imposed by an LLC's operating agreement. The agreement provided that a member could only transfer his complete ownership interest if the remaining member consented. In this case, the only two members were an individual and an S corporation that was solely owned by the *same* individual. The IRS determined that the individual controlled his S corporation—and the exercise of its consent—so that the purported consent restriction on transfer was not meaningful. As a result, the IRS disregarded the purported restriction and concluded that the LLC's interests were freely transferable.

Although the members in your LLC may desire a provision restricting the transferability of a membership interest to help reduce the risk that an LLC will be classified as a corporation, they may find a unanimous consent requirement undesirable. Although one alternative is that the transferee acquires governance interests only upon a vote of the majority of remaining members, it may also be possible to provide that the vote of only one or several members is required to approve such a transfer. Other degrees or forms of consent requirement may also be appropriate. Such tailormade standards are particularly desirable in family or closely held businesses and should be discussed with your adviser.

### Planning Tip 35

Consider using your operating agreement to specify a member's liability for withdrawing from an LLC as well as that of a new member who takes his or her place. Specify the following:

- Whether a withdrawing member is relieved of responsibility for all pre-existing debts

- Responsibility for future debts
- For which of these debts will a new member be responsible
- Whether a departing member will be indemnified for all or some of these obligations

Discuss the alternative forms of agreement with your advisers.

### Planning Tip 36

Consider the most efficient and effective means for limiting the transferability of membership interests in your LLC and, if desirable, include a provision in your operating agreement that satisfies your objectives.

### Entrepreneurs in Action

John Smith and Mike Harris agree that each can transfer his 50 percent membership interest in Smith Restaurants, LLC to family members or each other without limitation. A transfer to any other party will only involve the economic right to share in the profits and losses of the business, but not to participate in its management. For a transferee to acquire the right to participate in the LLC's management, the remaining member must provide his consent.

## Consequences of Disassociation by a Member

What happens when a member of an LLC withdraws as an owner? Withdrawal, sometimes referred to as a *disassociation,* can occur upon any event that causes a member to cease being a member. Common events precipitating a withdrawal are a sale of a membership interest and the bankruptcy or death of a member. Less common causes for withdrawal include the expulsion of a member or an adjudication that a member is legally incompetent.

LLC acts establish various consequences of disassociation by a member. In many states, a default rule provides that, if no agreement exists to the contrary, a member's disassociation will cause the dissolution of an LLC. As discussed in more detail in Chapter 10, an LLC can ordinarily be continued if an acceptable level of support to continue is reached by remaining members. Some states allow a member to withdraw without any limitation and, at such time, specify that the LLC must pay cash for his or her ownership interest. In other states, a member may only voluntarily withdraw if at least two-thirds of the remaining members consent. Your state may establish different rules. Providing that your LLC will be automatically terminated upon any member's disassociation is one way of ensuring that your LLC lacks the corporate characteristic of continuity of life. Tinkering with this general rule and seeking to limit its application, for example, by providing that only one designated member's disassociation will trigger a dissolution of the business, may result in the unintentional acquisition of continuity of life.

### Planning Tip 37

Use your operating agreement to establish—and restrict—the circumstances upon which a member may withdraw from your LLC as well as to specify the compensation to a withdrawing member, the form of that compensation (cash, property, etc.) and the time at which the compensation should be paid. Such tailormade restrictions may help prevent a withdrawing member from jeopardizing the availability of working capital by demanding a cash distribution immediately upon withdrawal. If the LLC had not anticipated the withdrawal, the demand could even force a liquidation of the business.

### Planning Tip 38

Discuss with your counsel how best to address the events and consequences of a member's disassociation while ensuring maintenance of partnership tax treatment.

### Entrepreneurs in Action

John and Mike agree that they must give each other at least 90 days' notice before withdrawing from their LLC. To further reduce the possibility that their withdrawal could unfairly hurt the business, they agree that their return of capital and other required distributions need not be made until 180 days from the date of withdrawal. Finally, they agree that if one of them dies, the LLC will be terminated unless the remaining member chooses to continue the business.

## Admission of New Members

Most state LLC acts distinguish between members who acquire their interest *when* the LLC is formed (an *initial member*) and members who acquire their interest *after* the LLC has been formed. Initial members acquire their interests directly from the LLC. Other members may acquire their interests from another member, not necessarily the LLC. An initial member is admitted on terms and conditions agreed to with the other founding members. The LLC acts vary in their provision for how others who seek a membership interest after the business has been established can do so without an agreement to the contrary. Some acts require the unanimous consent of the other members; others permit the admission of new members upon majority consent.

An operating agreement with rules for admitting new members can be useful if a state's applicable default rules are unacceptable. The agreement can specify the degree of consent required for admission—unanimous, majority or even less. Further, the agreement can establish qualifications for new members. Other possible restrictions or requirements include what form of notice of a proposed new member must be given to existing members or the waiting period before a prospective member is permitted to join the LLC.

### Entrepreneurs in Action

John and Mike decide they may wish to expand their business next year and bring in ten new members. They provide in the LLC operating agreement how the new members would be selected, how their ownership percentage would be established and what if any management rights the members could have.

## Trade Secrets and Confidential Information

How do you protect the confidential information or trade secrets of the business? An operating agreement can include provisions that restrict any or all members from divulging such information to any third party. It can even limit access to such information to designated members or managers only.

## Dispute Resolution

It is common for co-owners of a business to disagree about some aspect of their business relationship. Disagreements can be resolved quickly and easily or slowly and painfully. Many disagreements can fester and, ultimately, cause the collapse of a business. Although every disagreement is unique, some of the recurring business issues that cause disputes are the following:

- Whether member or employee salaries are too low or too high
- Whether business assets and opportunities are being misappropriated for personal use
- Whether one owner should be free to enter into a competing business
- The death of a key owner/employee
- Marital discord
- Disagreements about the value of an individual's contribution to a business

Although business owners typically agonize over their business plans, they often fail to consider how an internal dispute may affect their business. It is almost as if such businesspeople keep their fingers crossed and hope for the best.

Because the odds of avoiding a dispute are small, you should, among other things, think about how your operating agreement can minimize the damage caused when a dispute between members does occur. Although state LLC laws contain varying provisions as to rights of members and procedures to be followed if a dispute occurs, all states recognize that most of these rights and procedures can be augmented by agreement of the members. For example, although your state may permit a member to sue the LLC for alleged mismanagement (similar to a shareholder suing a corporation in a derivative suit), the members can establish a cheaper, more efficient, less public process to resolve such a dispute. Common mechanisms include using a neutral arbitrator or mediator, authorizing the buying and selling of ownership interests under specified terms and conditions or even appointing a designated outsider to manage the business if a dispute arises. These and other mechanisms could be included in your operating agreement, singly or in combination. As with other provisions, they should be periodically revisited to ensure that their terms remain relevant and acceptable to the current members.

### Entrepreneurs in Action

John and Mike are anxious that their business not be crippled if they have a serious disagreement. After considering many dispute resolution alternatives, they agree to submit their disputes to a neutrally appointed arbitrator whose decision will be both binding and nonappealable. Although they would prefer that their business decisions not be made by an outsider, they believe the arbitration process, if necessary, will be quicker, cheaper and less emotional than suing each other in court.

## Fiduciary Duties Members Owe to Each Other

A *fiduciary duty* refers to a particular obligation of trust or code of conduct that exists as a result of certain recognized relationships between individuals. Essentially, the relationship requires the individual with the duty to treat the party to whom the duty is owed fairly and in good faith. Sounds pretty vague, huh? I have to agree with you! Nevertheless, LLC acts generally require managers and, sometimes, members as well, to perform their duties in good faith and in compliance with standards applicable to fiduciaries.

Despite legal precedent on the standard of conduct required for members or managers to fulfill these duties, it can be helpful to define fiduciary obligations and their limits in your operating agreement. For example, you can provide that a member or manager is free or not free to enter into a contract with the LLC to provide certain products or services. Your operating agreement can state that a member or manager may not compete with the LLC. You can specify how certain duties should be interpreted and even identify activities that do or do not violate such duties. Your operating agreement can name the consequences for an individual who violates required standards of conduct. Finally, an operating agreement can provide that neither a member nor a manager shall owe any fiduciary duties to the LLC or other members except those required by law, such as the manager's duty to keep accurate books and records.

### Entrepreneurs in Action

John and Mike agree that, even though they are establishing a restaurant business together, either one of them is free to establish another restaurant or any other business without the other. They do agree, though, that such a restaurant should not offer substantially the same menu as the restaurant they will own and operate together. Thus, if Mike opens a restaurant across the street from the one he owns with John, with a different menu, John cannot complain that Mike has violated his duty to be loyal to the first restaurant business. As this example points out, higher or lower standards of care between LLC members may be good or bad, depending on whom you ask. Consider the possible consequences—both good and bad—of tinkering with these rules with your attorney.

## Partnership Tax Treatment Matters

Outside of the limited liability protection it offers its members, the potential for pass-through partnership tax treatment may be the most important feature in an LLC. A variety of issues are raised by this subject. Beyond the most fundamental question of which corporate characteristics an LLC will have (or not have) to ensure partnership tax classification, other questions with tax repercussions also arise. How will the LLC's income, profits, losses and deductions be allocated? Will such allocations have substantial economic effect? What are the tax consequences of a contribution or withdrawal of capital? What should the LLC's tax year be? Should the LLC use the cash or accrual method of accounting? Chapter 8 covers these and other questions. For now, note that when these questions have been answered, you may find it desirable or even necessary to specify the answers you and your co-owners reach in your operating agreement.

## Duration of LLC

Because the continuity of life characteristic plays such an important role in the tax structuring of an LLC, it is usually a good idea to address the contemplated duration of the business in an operating agreement. Recall that a business with a perpetual and continuous existence is considered to have continuity while a business whose life is limited in duration lacks this characteristic.

A number of state LLC acts contain default provisions limiting the life of an LLC to a particular term (often 30 years). Other LLC acts do not limit the term by statute but, instead, permit a limited life to be established by specifying a term of existence in an operating agreement. For example, a default provision in Wyoming's LLC act specifies that an LLC will be dissolved upon specified events, including the death or bankruptcy of a member unless the remaining members unanimously vote to continue the business. Such default provisions are usually unacceptable because they make planning difficult and offer little stability to the business. What can be done to improve planning opportunities and long-term stability? Consider including provisions in your operating agreement to narrow the likelihood of a business termination upon the occurrence of an event of dissolution. For example, although its tax consequences are still uncertain, you may find a pre-agreement to continue the business upon an event of dissolution to be a satisfactory approach. Limiting potential events of dissolution may be worth exploring. This subject is explored in greater detail in Chapter 10.

### Planning Tip 39

Early indications are that in order to ensure the lack of continuity of life and help avoid characterization as a corporation, your LLC's organizational documents should specify both an expiration date and the authority for members to dissolve the business before this date in specified circumstances. Without such authority, the mere designation of an expiration date may be insufficient to avoid a finding of continuity of life.

## Dissolution Events

A good operating agreement typically addresses the dissolution of the LLC under certain circumstances and the circumstances under which members of the LLC may choose to continue the business in spite of the dissolution.

Just as including a provision limiting the duration of your LLC in your articles of organization can cause uncertainty, so can specifying events of dissolution. This uncertainty is compounded if a unanimous vote of the remaining members to continue the business is required by agreement or by default. As discussed in Chapter 10, a number of techniques can reduce this uncertainty. One possibility is for the members to include in their operating agreement a provision that they all agree to continue the business if and when an event of dissolution occurs sometime in the future. Another technique is to provide in the operating agreement that a dissolution shall only occur if specified events (i.e., death, insanity, etc.) happen to one designated member of the LLC. You should consider these planning techniques only in consultation with your attorney.

### Winding Up and Termination

If an LLC is discontinued and the remaining members choose not to continue the business, the affairs of the LLC must be wound up and the business formally terminated. The winding up process refers to the orderly liquidation of assets, the payment of creditors' claims and, if applicable, the distribution of the remaining assets to the members of the LLC. Members of an LLC are usually well served to address a number of subjects relating to the winding up of the business in their operating agreement. For example, who winds up the LLC, members or managers? What if such individuals are responsible for the LLC's dissolution? See Chapter 10 for more detail on this subject.

# Issue Membership Certificates

Much like the share certificates issued by corporations, LLCs may issue membership certificates to evidence a member's ownership interest in the business. These certificates, which should be authorized by the LLC's operating agreement, may be pledged as security by a member unless the agreement prohibits the practice. If the LLC has limited the free transferability of its ownership interests, such limitations should be conspicuously noted on the membership certificate. Any purported sale of a membership interest in violation of a restriction noted on a certificate would be void.

### Entrepreneurs in Action

In order to place potential third party purchasers on notice of restrictions on the transferability of their LLC ownership interests, John and Mike type the following notation on the back of their respective membership certificates:

This certificate and the membership interested represented thereby are subject to the provisions of an operating agreement dated March 15, 1995, by and between John Smith, Mike Harris and Smith Restaurants, LLC (the LLC), whereby the sale, donation, assignment, encumbrance, collateralization, pledge, hypothecation, transfer or other disposition of such membership interest is restricted. A copy of said operating agreement is on file at the principal office of the LLC, where it may be inspected.

# CHAPTER 4

# Managing Your LLC Profitably

Effective decision making is a key ingredient of any successful business. Without good decision makers, issues about how profits should be allocated become moot. So do decisions about expansion, mergers and new business opportunities. Ultimately, even the complex and difficult issues involved in transferring a family-owned or closely held business from one generation to the next become academic. Yes, good decision making perpetuates a business; bad decision making kills it.

This chapter is devoted to the decision-making process in LLCs. Among the subjects covered are the roles members and managers play in an LLC, voting rights, annual meetings, quorum requirements, the election and removal of managers and officers and the authority members and managers have and the obligations they owe each other and the LLC. This chapter will not make a bad decision maker into a good one but it will reveal the tools that a good decision maker has to make his or her impact in running an LLC as significant as possible.

## Planning Tip 40

This chapter explores the planning options available for LLCs to structure firm management. Members, managers or a combination of both can manage an LLC. Before drafting your LLC's operating agreement to address the management responsibilities of members and, if applicable, managers, consider the default provisions of your state's LLC law. Some states say little on the subject while other states painstakingly detail such responsibilities.

Familiarizing yourself with the applicable default provisions will help you prepare an appropriate operating agreement.

## Management by Members

If there is no agreement between the members to the contrary, an LLC is managed by its members, who fill the same roles as shareholders, directors and officers of a corporation—at the same time. Members make the major decisions, such as mergers and dissolution, as well as more routine decisions, such as the compensation of the company's employees. Indeed, in theory, the members all have a vote on whether or not to buy new light bulbs for the business. In a member-managed LLC, the business avoids having the corporate characteristic of centralized management.

A member generally has the right to bind other members within an LLC. This authority may even extend to the execution of written documents that a member signs on behalf of the LLC. Under the legal doctrine of *apparent authority*, a member may bind an LLC to an obligation with another party if that party reasonably believes the member has authority (because of local custom, past practices of the LLC, etc.) even if the LLC's operating agreement specifically limits the member's authority. On the other hand, a member's act that is not apparently for the LLC's business or benefit will not bind the LLC unless otherwise authorized by the members.

### Entrepreneurs in Action

If John and Mike ignore the subject of who will be responsible for managing the affairs of their LLC, their applicable LLC act will provide that they are both equally responsible for management duties.

### Planning Tip 41

Experience suggests that the smaller the business, the easier it is to share management responsibility, while the bigger the business, the more important centralized management becomes. Although you will want to avoid having a majority of corporate characteristics in order to preserve your LLC's partnership tax treatment, consider providing centralized management to help run your business effectively.

### *Membership Voting*

States have generally taken one of two approaches to the mechanics of voting in a member-managed LLC. Perhaps the most common default provision on voting is that members vote in proportion to their current allocation of profits. This approach has the advantage of more accurately reflecting the economic interests of the membership but, on the down side, may present problems when valuing noncash capital contributions or adjusting values when capital is returned to its members as part of a distribution. An alternative to a capital contribution approach is a simple voting structure where each member has one vote, regardless of the ownership percentage. Decide whether your state's default provisions are acceptable and, if not, consider making a change in your LLC's operating agreement.

Many states set different threshold voting requirements for different issues. For example, a simple majority vote may be required for admitting a new member to an LLC while a two-thirds majority vote may be required to dissolve or merge the LLC. LLC acts may also contain alternative threshold voting requirements for amending an LLC's organizational documents, reducing or eliminating capital contributions, continuing the LLC after an event of dissolution and similar fundamental decisions.

### Planning Tip 42

Check the applicable voting standards in your state. If the default provisions are unacceptable, it may be possible to vary them in your operating agreement.

### Entrepreneurs in Action

John Smith has a 50 percent membership interest in Smith Restaurants, LLC. The other 50 percent is divided evenly between John's daughter, Jane (25 percent), and Mike Harris (25 percent). In a state that has a default provision based on proportion of ownership, Mike and Jane will each have one vote and John will have two. In another state, John, Jane and Mike could each have one vote.

## Meetings of Members

Unless otherwise prohibited by the articles of organization, members may generally either meet to consider and vote on taking action or, alternatively, consent to taking action in writing, without a formal meeting. If the latter occurs, which can often expedite the decision-making process, the written consent must be signed by members with the minimum number of votes needed to authorize the action if a meeting had been held.

### Planning Tip 43

Specify in your operating agreement such housekeeping matters as how much notice must be given to members before a meeting, whether participation by telephone or other communication equipment is acceptable and what constitutes a quorum to permit the transaction of business.

## Voting by Proxy

Sometimes a member finds it inconvenient to attend a meeting but wishes to vote on the issues under discussion. What's the answer? Consider permitting members to vote by proxy, which is a written authorization that one person gives to another so that the second person can represent and act on behalf of the first person. Many states specifically approve of the use of proxies by default; other states permit a member to vote by proxy if authorized by the LLC's operating agreement. If you do authorize the use of proxies, consider when they must be presented to the company and how long they will remain in effect. A member may wish to provide a proxy for one meeting, one issue, one year or longer. Of course, exercise care in tendering proxies with extended durations.

## Management by Fewer Than All Members

I can almost hear your groans! No business can be run by a committee of the whole! If every member can vote on even the most fundamental business decisions, nothing will ever be accomplished. Members will be preoccupied with making decisions and will have no time to get work done. I agree and, more importantly, so did the legislatures who enacted your state's LLC act.

Every LLC act allows members to delegate the management responsibilities of the business to one or more, but fewer than all, of the members. In effect, members may agree that their LLC should effectively have centralized management. If the members of an LLC wish to expand or restrict some or all of their management duties, they must do so in the articles of organization or operating agreement. There is virtually no limit to the number of ways management rights and responsibilities can be allocated among the members.

### Entrepreneurs in Action

To facilitate his estate planning objectives, John decides to gift portions of his ownership interest in Smith Restaurants, LLC, to his three children, Jim, John Jr., and Jane. In order to retain management control of the business, John has his children sign an operating agreement in which they agree that he shall be the only member with management responsibilities. This example of how LLCs can be used to help facilitate estate planning is addressed in more detail in Chapter 7.

## Retained Authority by Members

Even if the membership in an LLC opts to be centrally managed, most states still provide that the nonmanaging members retain authority to vote on certain fundamental decisions. For example, it is not unusual for an LLC act to require a majority of members to approve the following significant decisions:

- The sale or other disposition of substantially all of the LLC's assets
- The merger of the LLC with another business
- Incurring debt outside the ordinary course of business
- A change in the nature of the LLC's business
- Transactions involving conflicts of interest between members or managers and the LLC
- Amendment to the LLC's articles of organization or operating agreement

These, of course, are similar to the circumstances requiring approval by shareholders in a corporation or limited partners in a limited partnership. Outside of the foregoing retained authority, a nonmanaging member cannot assume management responsibility, nor can he or she serve as an agent with authority to bind the LLC, without an amendment to the LLC's articles of organization. A nonmanaging member, however, cannot inadvertently forfeit his or her limited liability protection. This contrasts with limited partners who, whether inadvertently or intentionally, can change their status (and, so, lose their limited liability protection) by merely participating in the management of their limited partnership.

### Entrepreneurs in Action

Although John, Jr., Jim and Jane Smith have delegated management of their LLC to their dad, if he seeks a bank loan to help finance the LLC's acquisition of a car dealership (i.e., something completely different from the restaurant business), dad will need his children's approval.

### Planning Tip 44

Depending on the flexibility of your state's LLC act, it may be possible to modify the extent of members' retained authority by an appropriate provision in your operating agreement.

## Indemnification of Members

LLC acts generally permit an LLC to indemnify its members against claims that arise in the ordinary course of business. Nonmanaging members may also be indemnified for certain monetary damages caused to the LLC. LLCs cannot, however, indemnify members for acts committed in bad faith, where a member has received an improper benefit or has breached a fiduciary duty to the other members or the LLC. Ordinarily, if an LLC wishes to indemnify its members, specific provision to that effect must be included in the LLC's operating agreement. Such protection is not typically provided by default.

### Planning Tip 45

Although it is expected that the *business judgment rule,* a presumption that a corporation's officers and directors have acted in good faith and for a proper business purpose, will be extended by statute or case law to apply to management decisions in LLCs, you can ensure its application by appropriate provision in your operating agreement.

## *Fiduciary Duties of Members*

Members are generally free to establish whatever standards of conduct for members they think reasonable; however, state LLC laws impose certain minimum standards. Although this area of law is not yet well developed and standards will likely vary by state, you will be safe to conclude that the relationship of members in an LLC to each other requires good faith and loyalty. Some states explicitly provide that members stand in a fiduciary relationship to each other. Other states are less explicit yet seem to accept this high standard of responsibility among members. Other states have concluded that members who are not also managers have no particular fiduciary or other duties to other members.

LLC members who, by default or by agreement, have management duties, are typically subject to fiduciary duties, including the duty to keep accurate books and records, the duty to render information to members, the duty of accountability and the duty not to self-deal. Nonmanaging members should also be presumed to owe certain fiduciary duties to other members. For example, nonmanaging members will presumably still owe a duty of loyalty to the LLC and a duty not to benefit personally from the business at the LLC's expense. It may be possible to limit or even eliminate some or all of these duties in your LLC by appropriate language in your operating agreement. Any attempt to alter otherwise applicable fiduciary duties should be done in consultation with your attorney.

An important subject between co-owners with unequal interests is what protection the minority interest owner has from being unfairly treated or oppressed by the majority owner. Although certain applicable fiduciary duties may regulate and help prevent unfair treatment, majority owners may nevertheless conform to otherwise acceptable conduct yet still outvote and oppress a minority member. Not all LLC acts specifically address the subject of unfair or oppressive treatment of some members by other members and you may wish to consider this subject with your attorney. States may be expected to borrow from their corporation laws on this subject.

State LLC acts may specify the consequences of a member's breach of fiduciary duty to the LLC. A common consequence is the expulsion of the member who acts improperly. Another consequence is to hold the member liable for financial damages caused by this conduct.

### Entrepreneurs in Action

John and Mike decide to eliminate the otherwise applicable duty of loyalty between themselves as members of the same LLC to permit either one of them to engage in unrelated restaurant businesses. Although they may choose not to compete, they are free to do so if a good opportunity comes along.

### Entrepreneurs in Action

John owns 80 percent of Smith Restaurants, LLC; Mike owns the remaining 20 percent. John decides to employ two of his children, John, Jr., and Jimmy, in the business. He starts them off with substantial salaries, which he increases on a periodic basis. As a result of these increases, the LLC's distributions to Mike decrease. Although Mike voices his concern to John, the children's salaries continue to rise. If the LLC's operating agreement doesn't provide appropriate protection, Mike's only remedy may be to seek a judicial dissolution of the business.

### Planning Tip 46

Consider including in your operating agreement specific procedures to follow, or standards of conduct to adhere to, to reduce the occurrence or consequences of member oppression.

### Planning Tip 47

Review your state LLC act's provisions about fiduciary duties and the consequences for disregarding such duties. If appropriate, consider specifying additional consequences in your LLC's operating agreement.

## Management by Managers

LLC acts authorize the management of an LLC by one or more managers. The managers may, but need not be members of the business. A manager can be an individual, corporation, another LLC or other legal entity. If this management feature is desired, the articles of organization must provide that such a feature is permissible. A variety of different management structures can be created in an LLC. For example, a manager-managed LLC could still permit nonmanager members to bind the LLC. Alternatively, a member-managed LLC could be structured so that nonmanager members cannot bind the LLC. If an LLC is managed by managers, it will ordinarily possess the corporate characteristic of centralized management. Because some of the possible management structures may be deemed to create centralized management and some may not, the safest course is to review your structure with your attorney.

### Planning Tip 48

Use your LLC's operating agreement to specify, among other things, any qualifications a manager must have, the number of managers and the terms of their respective appointments, which may vary between managers, grounds for removal and the responsibilities of each management position. Determine how a manager's compensation is to be fixed. Under many LLC acts, unless otherwise provided by the members in their operating agreement, managers have the authority to fix their own salaries!

### Planning Tip 49

In a business transaction (such as acquisition of a business or bank financing), the outside party (e.g., the seller or bank) should know who has signing authority to bind the business. To confirm the LLC's legal existence, compliance with its state LLC act and its authority to enter into a specific transaction, you may wish to supply the following:

- A certified copy of your LLC's articles of organization
- A certified copy of its operating agreement
- A certificate copy of a good standing certificate (furnished by the state office in charge of LLC filings)
- Resolutions authorizing the transaction and the manager's authority to enter into a particular transaction

## Management Decision Making

Unless otherwise provided by the articles of organization or operating agreement, each manager (if there is more than one) typically has one vote and management decisions require majority approval. If the management of an LLC is vested in one or more managers, the members generally relinquish their authority to bind the LLC. Instead, with limited exceptions, only the managers have such authority. An exception arises if the manager's authority has been limited in certain circumstances and the person who seeks to bind the LLC based on the manager's actions knew or should have known that the manager's authority was limited.

In order to place some restrictions on a manager's authority, the members of an LLC may include *negative covenants* in their operating agreement. Examples of negative covenants are restrictions on a manager's ability to undertake the following:

- Pay salaries to employees in excess of specified levels
- Borrow or spend money in excess of specified amounts
- Sell a substantial part of the LLC's assets without prior approval from the members
- Enter a new line of business

If you include such restrictions on a manager's ability, consider its impact on the presence of centralized management. Presumably, the more restrictions imposed on a manager, the less likely it is that the LLC will be determined to have centralized management.

### Planning Tip 50

In structuring your LLC to ensure partnership tax treatment, avoid the characteristic of centralized management through member management. If the use of managers is considered essential, consider having the members retain certain authority, such as decision-making authority on personnel matters or check writing authority. This will permit you to argue to the IRS (especially if the operating agreement contains a number of restrictive covenants on the manager's authority) that the LLC lacks centralized management despite having a manager.

### Planning Tip 51

If you are uncertain whether your management structure meets the threshold for centralized management, consider requesting guidance from the IRS by a private letter ruling.

## Classes of Managers

An LLC's flexibility permits the use of different classes of managers with different rights and responsibilities to the LLC. For example, management classes can be differentiated on the basis of their right to vote on certain issues or the subject of their management authority (e.g., sales, manufacturing, administration, etc.). The possible distinctions are limited only by the members' imagination and good business sense. The operating agreement should specify any distinction in management classes.

## Management by Officers

The membership of an LLC may decide that, instead of giving two or more managers an equal vote in the decision-making process, a hierarchy of power should be established. No problem. The members can provide in their articles of organization or operating agreement that certain managers have more authority than others. Many LLC acts even expressly permit the use of officer titles, such as president, vice-president, secretary and treasurer, so that management power can be delegated in accordance with the traditional scheme of authority found in corporations. Most LLC acts are flexible with respect to management issues and the formalities of compliance. LLCs are generally free to keep their management structure relatively loose and unstructured or, if preferred, extremely structured, with traditional formalities such as the use of proxies, notice, place and time of meetings, etc.

### Planning Tip 52

If you choose to appoint officers, consider specifying in your operating agreement the duties of each officer, terms of office, compensation (unless it will be determined at the discretion of a manager) and how officers are elected and, perhaps, removed.

### Planning Tip 53

Decide what degree of organizational formality works best for your business and prepare your operating agreement to reflect your preference.

## Fiduciary Duties of Managers

Although members are generally free to establish the roles and standards of conduct for managers they think reasonable, state LLC laws impose certain minimum standards of conduct. For example, managers are required by law to perform their duties in good faith and with the same degree of care that an ordinarily prudent person would exercise in similar circumstances. Most LLC acts explicitly or implicitly impose the same types of fiduciary duties on managers that state law imposes on officers and directors of a corporation. Under a duty of loyalty, a manager is required to act in the LLC's best interests, not the manager's. On occasion, a manager is in a position to take action on behalf of the LLC in a manner that is personally beneficial. Can he or she do so? The general rule is yes, *if* the manager has disclosed the opportunity to the other managers or, if none, to the members and they approve of the action.

Managers, like directors in a corporation, are generally permitted to rely on the reports, opinions or statements prepared by others in discharging their duties. Such reports may be prepared by reliable employees or agents of the LLC, professional advisers to the LLC (attorneys, accountants, bankers, etc.) or even a management committee on which the manager does not serve. Of course, as with directors and officers, a manager who knows or should know that such reports or statements are unreliable is not permitted to use them. A manager who does use unreliable information may be held liable for losses caused to the business. Managers in LLCs may be called to account for certain losses incurred by the business as a result of their misconduct, as may their counterparts in other forms of business. For example, a manager who uses confidential information acquired during service to the LLC for personal benefit and to the detriment of the LLC may be called to account for the damages and held responsible for the loss. Even a broad right of indemnification will not insulate a manager from such claims.

### Planning Tip 54

To avoid confusion and prevent divided loyalties, members should consider adopting a general rule that prohibits any business dealings between managers and the LLC.

## Management Liability and Indemnification

Unfortunately, it is not unheard of for a business to lose money. Any number of causes may be responsible for the loss: changes in consumer preferences, rising costs of key ingredients or cheaper labor overseas, to name but a few. Notwithstanding perfectly rational explanations to establish that no one is to blame for such losses, owners of the business, inevitably, seek to point fingers. The party most likely to be accused is the manager who is calling the shots.

Businesses and individuals can also lose money as a result of an unsuccessful transaction with another business. Often, the loss is caused by a breach of contract: A business makes a commitment that it is unable to live up to. Product is ordered, and the invoice cannot be paid. Material is produced that is defective. The list in our litigious society could go on endlessly. The business or individual sustaining a significant loss will consider pursuing a claim against the responsible business. Depending on the circumstances and the litigation strategy, the aggrieved party may also assert a claim against the manager of the business responsible for the loss.

Claims against managers in these and other circumstances often have no merit and are asserted primarily to secure psychological or tactical advantages against an opponent. Nevertheless, the manager is forced to defend the suit to prevent the entry of a judgment against him or her, often at substantial expense.

To provide a measure of protection, incentives to take appropriate risks and financial security, many businesses agree to indemnify their managers. Most LLC acts authorize LLC members to indemnify managers for a wide variety of claims, often as broadly as their counterpart corporate law authorizes the indemnification of officers and directors. To provide such indemnification to a manager, the LLC's operating agreement should specify the existence and scope of its protection.

Notwithstanding an LLC's ability to indemnify its managers, there are limits. The typical LLC act precludes an LLC from indemnifying a manager who has breached a fiduciary duty to the business or its members, has received an improper benefit from the LLC or is guilty of fraud, bad faith or intentional misconduct. Provisions of an operating agreement that purport to excuse a manager in even these circumstances may be disregarded.

### Planning Tip 55

Because a right to indemnification is of little value if the party being indemnified has to wait to be reimbursed until after the final disposition of a claim, consider providing in your operating agreement that a manager or member who is being indemnified by the company shall be paid or reimbursed for reasonable expenses from time to time and in advance of a final disposition of the claim. Your agreement can also provide that any amount advanced should be repaid if the individual is ultimately determined not to be entitled to indemnification.

### *Election*

Except as the members may otherwise provide in their operating agreement, many LLC acts provide that the election of managers by the members shall occur annually. If desirable, you can provide in your operating agreement that a manager holds the position for a shorter, longer or even unlimited period of time. The LLC's flexibility even permits the appointment of different managers for differing periods.

### *Removal*

Unless otherwise provided in an LLC's operating agreement, any manager can ordinarily be replaced or removed without establishing just cause by vote of a majority in interest of the LLC members. If you prefer to limit the circumstances that will justify a manager's removal, specify such limits in your operating agreement.

### Resignation

Depending on the term of the operating agreement and/or any applicable employment agreement, a manager may be free to resign with or without notice, only upon specified notice or, perhaps, strictly prohibited from resigning and even be liable to the LLC for a wrongful resignation. In the latter event, the LLC could recover any damages directly caused as a result of the unauthorized resignation. If such claims would be unwelcome, consider including a provision in your applicable agreements authorizing a manager to resign, perhaps after giving appropriate notice to the LLC.

### Annual Meeting of Members

Most state LLC acts provide that a meeting of all members of an LLC will occur at least once a year. This is similar to the requirement for annual meetings of shareholders of corporations and is intended to ensure that owners remain updated on the affairs of the business. Minutes of the meeting should ordinarily be taken to document the nature of the discussion. Although such meetings are usually important, some states permit members to dispense with this requirement for their LLCs. An appropriate provision in the operating agreement to that effect should accomplish the dispensation.

#### Planning Tip 56

Consider the mechanical issues that arise in planning and holding annual or other meetings of members and include appropriate provisions in your LLC's operating agreement. For example, specify the following:

- Who calls the annual or other meeting(s) of members
- How much advance notice needs to be given before a meeting
- How such notice is given (e.g., by telephone, mail, fax, etc.)
- Who sets the agenda for the meeting and how meetings are adjourned

By specifying the procedure you and the other members wish to follow, you can help reduce the likelihood of a dispute.

## Operational Considerations

### Suits by and against the LLC

Ordinarily, neither a member nor a manager of an LLC is liable for the debts or obligations of the LLC or each other. This protection extends to claims for breach of contract, personal injury and other matters. As a consequence of this general rule, a member or manager is ordinarily *not* a proper party to a claim brought by or against an LLC. Such suits should be maintained by the LLC or defended by the LLC as may be appropriate. The authority to bring a suit on its own account rests with those individuals who have requisite management authority to do so.

### Planning Tip 57

Be sure to comply with applicable formation and/or registration requirements in your LLC's home state (or in a foreign state it is doing business in) so that, among other things, your LLC will be able to begin a lawsuit.

## Firm Liability for Members' Actions

Although the *members* of an LLC may be protected in their individual capacity from certain claims under the doctrine of limited liability, the *business* itself is responsible for its own debts and obligations and can even be held responsible for certain wrongful acts of one or more, but fewer than all, members. For example, if a member negligently injures someone while engaged in an activity on behalf of the LLC, the business may be liable. States have varying statutory or common law provisions on the extent that a business may be held culpable for acts of members. In a few states (as is the case with corporations), it may even be possible for an LLC to be held criminally responsible for the illegal conduct of its members. Members withdrawing from an LLC may remain responsible for particular firm liabilities existing as of the date of withdrawal. To avoid liability for future obligations, among other things, creditors of the LLC should be notified of the departure.

### Planning Tip 58

It is sometimes possible for an exiting member to enter into an agreement with the LLC that limits the member's liability to debts and obligations existing at the time of departure. Consider the desirability of such an agreement for your case.

## Liability of Incoming Members

In the absence of an agreement to the contrary, a new member of an existing LLC has no special protection from the debts and obligations that arose before his or her admission. As a result, a new member's capital contributions are available to satisfy outstanding obligations. This result, nevertheless, is an improvement on the status of an incoming partner to a partnership who, without the benefit of limited liability protection, could be held personally liable for such pre-existing obligations.

## Operating Your LLC in Other States

What must you do to operate your LLC in a state other than the one in which your company is organized? This question is now answered more easily because of the recent enactment of legislation in most states authorizing the use of LLCs. Most LLC acts include specific registration provisions that should be followed by *foreign LLCs* (i.e., LLCs formed in other states or other countries) wishing to transact business in their state. Typically, these acts specify what constitutes the transaction of business and, so, when registration procedures must be followed. The process typically requires an LLC to file an application with a secretary of state or other designated official for a certificate of authority to transact business in that state. The procedure, which is neither expensive nor complicated, resembles the one followed by a corporation that seeks to qualify to do business in a foreign state.

An LLC that neglects the foreign registration process is ordinarily precluded from bringing a legal proceeding in that state until it complies. Most states provide that the state law under which an LLC has been organized continues to apply in their jurisdiction. Many states, however, will not permit foreign LLCs to operate in a manner or for a purpose that is not available to their domestic LLCs. Also, in many states, a foreign LLC's members' and managers' rights can be no greater than the rights available to domestic members and managers.

It is unclear how a state that has not adopted LLC legislation will treat foreign LLCs. Many issues exist, from how title to property held by an LLC will be held to whether the members' limited liability will be respected. There are no easy answers, although the importance of this issue has diminished with the passage of LLC legislation in most states.

### Planning Tip 59

Before operating in another state, consider that state's LLC law to determine how your business will be treated under its laws.

## Recordkeeping Requirements

States have long recognized that a business can only be managed if its managers have access to relevant information. Accordingly, numerous laws, varying from state to state, establish the kind of books, records and other information that must be kept by general and limited partnerships as well as by corporations. Most LLC acts also require that certain business information be maintained and available for inspection, such as a current list of all members with their last known business address, copies of tax returns, a statement of each member's capital contributions, a copy of the operating agreement and rights of members to make or receive distributions. You should consider the applicable recordkeeping requirements in your jurisdiction.

## Bank Accounts

As with any other business, the LLC requires a decision about where to keep its bank accounts and investment accounts. The operating agreement should state which member(s) or manager(s) will be authorized to withdraw funds and make investment decisions. To avoid confusion and related problems, the agreement should also specify that the LLC's funds are not to be commingled with any other funds, including the personal funds of any member or manager.

### Planning Tip 60

When opening a bank account, make sure that the designated member(s) or manager(s) in charge of banking relations have a taxpayer identification number, a copy of the LLC's articles of organization and, if requested, a copy of the operating agreement and resolutions from the members or managers, as applicable, authorizing the opening of the account.

## LLCs in Bankruptcy

The treatment of LLCs under the Bankruptcy Code is somewhat uncertain because the code does not specifically refer to LLCs as a type of debtor that is eligible for protection. Nevertheless, many experts believe that LLCs may be considered either a "person" or (less likely) a "corporation" as those terms are defined in the code and, so defined, be eligible for relief as a debtor. Given the increasing popularity of the LLC form, it is difficult to believe that the bankruptcy laws will not be expressly extended to ensure protection of LLCs. More definitive guidance can be expected shortly.

### Planning Tip 61

Consider including in your LLC's operating agreement provisions to ensure efficient use of the protection from claims offered by the bankruptcy laws. For example, consider specifying the following: (1) who has or doesn't have authority to file a petition for relief under the code and (2) whether the managers who operated the business before the bankruptcy remain in place or whether new managers should be selected. Anticipating these types of questions now can help reduce confusion and problems later.

## Members in Bankruptcy

Like the treatment of LLCs in bankruptcy, the effect of an LLC member's bankruptcy remains somewhat uncertain, although guidance from the legal system can be expected shortly. The confusion stems from the fact that LLC acts typically contain default provisions requiring the dissolution of an LLC upon a member's bankruptcy. (Of course, as discussed in Chapter 10, the business could then be continued upon agreement of two or more remaining members.) Under the bankruptcy law, however, a debtor has authority to assume or reject certain *executory contracts* (i.e., contracts that contemplate further performance in the future). Potentially, an LLC's operating agreement could be considered such a contract. Thus, in theory, a debtor could choose to assume the LLC's operating agreement and thereby avoid the automatic dissolution of the LLC. A debtor could even argue that he or she should be able to continue to exercise management responsibility, if applicable. This result may or may not be desirable from the perspective of the LLC as well as that of the other members. How, in fact, a member's bankruptcy will affect an LLC and the member must be clarified by the courts or state legislatures.

# CHAPTER 5

# Financing Your LLC

Although, by now, you may think LLCs possess magical qualities, they have their limits. LLCs, for example, cannot make money grow on trees! Like other business forms, however, LLCs can be financed with debt, equity, venture capital, SBA loans and other means. You can use your personal resources as well as capital from friends, family, banks and other financial institutions. You will learn in this chapter how the inherent flexibility of an LLC can be used strategically to help raise money for your LLC as well as address and resolve many financial issues that arise in the course of business. Can a business that is unable to raise money as a partnership or corporation raise money as an LLC? Probably not, because most investors or lenders will focus on the business opportunity and the strength of the management team. On the other hand, by forming your business as an LLC, you make such features as flexible returns, management influence and limited liability available to numerous sources of capital. Also, your use of an LLC may reflect a desirable level of sophistication to potential sources of capital. Let's begin with the first financial issue you will face, raising the initial capital for your business from its members.

### Planning Tip 62

As with other businesses, in financing your LLC, evaluate the possible consequences of mixing sources of money—the debt-equity ratio. Although debt can produce high rates of return, the consequences of not repaying a loan are much more traumatic than those of not paying a dividend to an equity owner or, in the case of an LLC, not making a distribution to a member. Consider the optimum mix of available capital with your adviser.

### Planning Tip 63

Identify yourself as an individual who is able to seize on new opportunities by forming an LLC—or noting to a prospective lender that you at least have considered its use—and watch your reputation help you to raise needed money!

## Capital Contributions

LLC acts generally provide that anything of value can be used to finance a business. The most typical capital contributions are, as in other forms of business, cash, property (both real and personal), services or a promise to contribute one of these at some time in the future. In some jurisdictions, if a creditor has a claim against an LLC whose resources are insufficient to satisfy the claim, the creditor may seek to enforce a member's promise to make a capital contribution in the future. The member may be unable to shield himself or herself against such a claim by asserting the limited liability protection otherwise offered by the LLC. Bottom line: The member may be required to make the payment.

As we will explore in Chapter 8, a member who transfers property for a membership interest in an LLC has technically sold that property to the LLC. Such a sale would ordinarily require the member to recognize a capital gain or loss. Under applicable federal partnership tax rules, however, the contributing member's gain or loss is not reported. When the LLC subsequently sells the contributed asset, the amount and character of the gain or loss will be determined as if the member had sold the asset individually.

### Entrepreneurs in Action

John and Mike form an LLC. In addition to cash and management construction services, Mike agrees to contribute a professional-style stove to their LLC as his initial contribution. The stove has a basis of $2,000 and a fair market value of $10,000. The members agree to increase Mike's capital account by $10,000 as a result of his contribution of the stove. If the LLC replaces the stove next year, and is able to sell it for $6,000, then the LLC will recognize a capital gain of $4,000 (the sale price of $6,000 less contributor's basis of $2,000 = $4,000 gain).

### Planning Tip 64

If a contribution is made in a form other than cash, the members are advised to agree, in writing and at the time the contribution is made, what the contribution is worth.

### Planning Tip 65

Consider including a provision in your operating agreement that permits the substitution of one form of capital for another in the event of hardship or impossibility. For example, if Mike Harris promises to provide construction services worth $200,000 to Smith Restaurants, LLC, but his workforce is on strike, it may or may not be sufficient if he contributes $200,000 cash instead.

### Planning Tip 66

Consider specifying in your operating agreement the consequences to a member who fails to make a required capital contribution. Some, but not all, possible consequences could include the reduction, elimination or the forced sale of the defaulting member's ownership interest in the LLC.

## Capital Accounts

An LLC should maintain a record of the value of each member's equity in the business. This record is commonly referred to as a *capital account*. When the business is formed, the capital account records each member's investment in the LLC. Capital accounts should, thereafter, be adjusted to reflect each member's receipts of distributions, additional capital contributions to the LLC and allocable share of income and loss.

### Planning Tip 67

With your accountant, consider revaluing your LLC's capital accounts in certain circumstances. For example, there may be occasions when unrealized gains or losses should be treated for accounting purposes as if they had, in fact, been realized.

## Capital Shortfalls

It is usually a good idea to specify any requirements for members to make additional contributions of capital to the LLC following initial contributions. Additional capital is often required to develop or maintain a company's operations. The managers may have used their best efforts to eliminate the need for capital, or even to secure commercially reasonable loans, all to no avail. What then? One option is to authorize a procedure allowing the manager(s) to seek additional funds from each member on a voluntary basis. For example, the manager could send a written request to each member, asking for an additional capital contribution in the amount of the member's pro-rata share of the capital shortfall. If necessary funds are not raised, the manager could again ask the members who did contribute for even more money, perhaps as a loan or in return for an increased equity position in the business. In some operating agreements, members have even provided that a failure to make a requested contribution automatically creates a debt from the member to the LLC in the requested amount, which accrues interest until paid.

A member of an LLC may seek to increase his or her ownership interest by making additional capital contributions that, because of disparate financial circumstances, other members would be unable to make. This scenario frequently occurs in other forms of business as well. Many techniques are available, for example, to shareholders of corporations who wish to prevent the unfair dilution of their ownership interests. Because it is often difficult to foresee future events and circumstances, your LLC's operating agreement could state that no member shall be required to make additional capital contributions without the (unanimous) consent of the members.

### Planning Tip 68

A variety of the antidilution techniques commonly available to shareholders should also be available to members of LLCs. Consider including one or more such provisions in your operating agreement. A simple provision, for example, might state that a member shall not be permitted to make an additional capital contribution without the (unanimous) consent of the members.

## Allocation of Profits and Losses

Typically, when there is no agreement to the contrary, the LLC's profits and losses are distributed equally among the members, regardless of their capital contributions. Some states, however, provide that the allocation of profits and losses should be made according to the member's capital interest. The members are free to override a state's default provisions and allocate the profits and losses of their business as they choose. The members' flexibility in this regard is significant, perhaps limited only by applicable tax requirements that such allocations be reasonable. Among other things, for example, members may allocate profits one way and losses a completely different way. They may provide for preferential allocations of profits to some members before others, the preferential allocation of tax benefits to some members and not others or even for amending the allocation formula upon the occurrence of agreed-upon events.

A limited number of technical exceptions created by the tax law restrict an LLC's freedom to allocate profits and losses among its members in any manner that is agreeable. For example, one restriction prohibits the LLC from assigning income to a member if the income was actually earned before that member's admission into the LLC. There is, perhaps, no more important understanding between the members than this one. Be smart! Put your understanding in writing—in your operating agreement—to help avoid future disputes!

### Entrepreneurs in Action

In a state allocating profits and losses based on membership interests, if John's capital interest is $60,000 and Mike's is $40,000, they would, in the absence of an agreement to the contrary, share in the profits and losses on a 60-40 basis, respectively.

### Planning Tip 69

Some important restrictions on allocations are discussed in Chapter 8. Consult your attorney when making special allocations of an LLC's income, deductions, gains and losses to avoid unanticipated tax consequences.

### Entrepreneurs in Action

Smith Restaurants, LLC's income is due to the efforts of John and Mike. If these members seek to reduce their tax liability and allocate their income to their children, they may be precluded from doing so by a tax rule prohibiting the assignment of partnership income to a partner (member) who did not render the services that generated the income.

## Distributions of Capital

LLCs may distribute some or all of their assets to their members, with limited exceptions. These distributions can be made in the normal course of an ongoing business, like a dividend from a corporation, upon the winding up of the business affairs or when a member relinquishes an ownership interest in an LLC by either voluntary withdrawal or expulsion. Cash or tangible assets can be used for distributions. Unless otherwise authorized to do so in an operating agreement, a member cannot generally compel the LLC to make a distribution in any form other than cash. By the same token, an LLC cannot generally compel its members to accept more than a pro-rata share of a noncash distribution. Consider these generally applicable limitations on distributions of capital when you organize your LLC. A tailormade provision could be more desirable for your circumstance.

## Limits on Distributions

Although provisions vary from state to state, most LLC acts limit when distributions can be made. If one of these applicable limitations does not apply, a distribution is permitted. The most common limitations provide that a distribution cannot be made: (1) if its effect would render the LLC unable to pay its debts as they become due, (2) if it would leave the LLC insolvent (i.e., with more liabilities than assets) and (3) if it is precluded by the terms of the LLC's articles of organization or operating agreement. A member or manager who is responsible for authorizing an improper distribution may face personal liability to the LLC's creditors to the extent of their financial injury. A manager, of course, may be held harmless if the decision to authorize a distribution was reasonably made in reliance on the company's financial statements. Similarly, any member who receives an improper distribution may be required to reimburse the LLC for the prohibited amount received.

## Distributions in the Course of Business

Except for the foregoing limitations, an LLC is otherwise free to make distributions to its members in accordance with the provisions of its articles of organization or operating agreement. Such distributions typically occur in the form of regular draws, distributions of profit and return of capital. LLCs, which have no limit on the number and types of ownership classes that can be established, can be structured to allocate distributions in any variety of ways. This flexibility suggests another advantage of LLCs over S corporations, which are permitted to issue only one class of stock. Ordinarily, in the absence of an agreement to the contrary, distributions from LLCs to members are allocated on the basis of the value of their membership interests.

### Planning Tip 70

Discuss standards for distributions with fellow members of your LLC and incorporate your decision in the LLC's operating agreement at the inception of the business to avoid disputes. Address not only the fair allocation of distributions, but the standard for when distributions can be made.

## Distributions upon Voluntary Withdrawal

A member may relinquish his or her ownership interest and voluntarily withdraw from an LLC under certain circumstances as provided in the applicable LLC act or organizational documents. Voluntary withdrawals generally include retirement, agreement to withdraw as part of the resolution of a dispute with the LLC or its remaining members and agreement between the estate of a deceased LLC member and the LLC. Most acts also permit a member to withdraw after giving appropriate notice to the other members.

If a member voluntarily withdraws from an LLC, some states provide that the member is entitled to receive a payment equal to the value the interest would have if the LLC were terminated and its obligations paid, such value to be determined as of the date of withdrawal. Instead of using what amounts to an assumed liquidation value, other states establish the value of a member's interest by assuming that the business is an ongoing concern. An ongoing-concern valuation is nearly always higher than a liquidation valuation and requires the LLC to distribute more capital to the withdrawing member. Accordingly, you should specify how a withdrawing member's interest will be calculated in your LLC's operating agreement.

LLCs can have an unlimited number of members, while S corporations can have no more than 35 shareholders. Nevertheless, use of LLCs for businesses with many members may become unwieldy if any member's withdrawal automatically terminates the business unless the remaining members unanimously consent to continuing the business. Without contingency plans, unexpected member withdrawals could sap the business of needed capital. To address these issues, explore the possibility of not only overriding the unanimous consent requirement by using a simple majority or even a single designated member or manager, but also of precluding any member from receiving a capital distribution until passage of an agreed-upon amount of time. You should also consider the amount of notice a withdrawing member must give before being permitted to withdraw. Sudden withdrawals can impair the financial strength of an LLC because of the need to make a distribution of capital to the withdrawing member. Also, in more complex situations, consider forming an LLC whose members are made up of S corporations or limited partners, which do not dissolve on the withdrawal of each shareholder or limited partner.

### Planning Tip 71

Your LLC's operating agreement should address how to determine the value of a withdrawing member's interest, including the merits of using commonly accepted valuation discounts (for minority ownership, lack of marketability, etc.), penalties for withdrawal under certain circumstances and other such matters. Your state's default rules on withdrawal may not be satisfactory for your situation.

### Distributions upon a Member's Expulsion

LLCs are free to set their own rules on when a member should be expelled or forced to withdraw as an owner in the business. Many LLCs provide in their operating agreement that a member can be expelled for breach of fiduciary duty, breach of the company's operating agreement or related circumstances.

Members are also free to specify in their operating agreement what distribution an expelled member is entitled to receive. When there is no such agreement, a typical default provision requires the LLC to make the same distribution to an expelled member as it would make to a voluntarily departing member, subject to an offset for such damages as the expelled member has inflicted on the LLC.

### Distributions upon Dissolution of the Business

As discussed in more detail in Chapter 10, an LLC may, for any number of reasons, cease doing business and wind up its affairs. In this case, the LLC sells off its assets, settles its obligations with creditors and distributes its remaining assets to its members. If sufficient assets remain for the members, they are distributed according to the provisions of the operating agreement or, if no agreement has been reached, as provided in the applicable default provisions.

## Assignment of Membership Interests

Most businesspeople agree that the ability to transfer ownership interests freely is a desirable feature that can help a business attract capital. Investors often desire the freedom to cash out and hesitate to invest if they can't readily exit from the business. On the other hand, most business owners prefer to choose their partners and not have strangers foisted upon them as partners. This interest is usually best served in family-owned and closely held businesses by establishing restrictions on the transfer of an ownership interest, at least without the consent of other owners.

An LLC can help comfortably accommodate these sometimes competing objectives. Most LLC acts contain default provisions that permit a member to assign his or her ownership interest to another party. Because, however, an unrestricted right to transfer a membership interest in an LLC may be deemed to constitute the corporate characteristic of free transferability, many acts authorize a member to transfer a financial, but not a governance, interest in the LLC without agreement by the other members. A financial interest generally refers to a member's right to share in profits, losses and distributions of the LLC. A governance interest, by contrast, encompasses all of a member's other, nonfinancial, rights, including the right to participate in the management of the LLC. In many ways, this rule is a nice accommodation of the varying interests. An investor can exit the business, if desired, by selling his or her membership interest to an outsider. The remaining members, however, are not generally required to work closely with the new member and can continue to operate the business as they choose. They can simply make those distributions to the new member that the old member was previously entitled to receive.

### Planning Tip 72

States have established varying consent requirements relating to the assignment of a member's governance interests (e.g., unanimous or majority consent required). However, states with flexible acts may permit their default provisions to be varied by appropriate provision in an operating agreement. If you do so, be careful to consider its effect on the presence or absence of free transferability.

### Entrepreneurs in Action

John and Mike have been in business together for several years. Now, Mike would like to cash out, move to Florida and retire. John would like to stay in business but he can't afford to buy out Mike's share of the LLC. Mike approaches his cousin, Henry Dimwitty. Henry inherited a sizeable fortune from his parents, which is a good thing because Henry is not very smart. Mike can sell his ownership interest to Henry and get the cash he needs. Henry will be entitled to the same financial rights that Mike previously had. John isn't too disappointed. Although he doesn't respect Henry's business skills, he doesn't need to worry because Mike could not transfer his governance interest in the LLC to Henry without John's consent.

# Compensation of Members and Managers

As noted in the prior chapter, depending upon the agreement of the members, one or more, or even all, of the members may be compensated by the LLC. Although the subject of compensation is generally not explicitly addressed in LLC acts, all acts permit an LLC to retain managers and employees to help operate the business. This authority impliedly permits the members to compensate such individuals. Indeed, LLCs may provide more flexibility in structuring and modifying, when appropriate, compensation packages for key employees than is available to S corporations. For example, in an LLC, compensation can easily be adjusted by amending an operating agreement. In S corporations, by contrast, there may be a need to redeem and retire stock, then issue new stock. Such machinations can be awkward, complex and expensive. In some states such as New York, an exception to the limited liability afforded by a corporation provides that certain shareholders are personally liable for unpaid employee wages. This can be a huge liability to any such shareholder of a company that is forced to close its doors. By contrast, an informal survey suggests that states do not impose similar personal liability on members of LLCs. Advantage, again, to the LLC!

### Planning Tip 73

Use your LLC's flexibility to establish salaries in any reasonable way that is acceptable to the members.

## Application of Federal Securities Laws to LLCs

The Securities and Exchange Commission (SEC) regulates the marketing, purchase and sale of select securities. The goal of the federal securities laws is to protect investors from unfair and deceptive practices and to promote full disclosure about businesses that issue securities. Securities are defined by federal law to include such familiar forms of interest as stock, notes, bonds, debentures, options and *investment contracts*. More esoteric ownership interests in businesses are also considered securities.

A membership interest in an LLC has not yet been explicitly included in the definition of a security. Nevertheless, the applicability of the federal securities laws to LLCs must be considered on a case-by-case basis whenever membership interests are sold because of the possibility that a membership interest can be characterized as an investment contract. In a case captioned *SEC v. J. Howey Company*, the United States Supreme Court explained that an investment contract is a transaction in which a person "invests his money in a [business] and is led to expect profits solely from the efforts of [others]." This test was later broadened when the requirement that the profits be "solely" from the efforts of others was modified so that all that is required is that profits be "substantially" from the efforts of others.

Although no case has yet been decided that finds a membership interest to be a form of investment contract, it is very possible that the federal securities law, which makes a distinction on the basis of whether an investor is "active" or "passive," could encompass membership interests. The determining factor may be the roles members play in the management of the business. For example, if an LLC with over a thousand members is centrally managed by two or three managers, the members are "passive investors" and, much like similar interests of limited partners, their interests may well be deemed appropriate for regulation under the securities laws. If, on the other hand, an LLC has only three members, each with an equal voice in management, their membership interests are more "active" and thus less likely to be regulated.

Moreover, an LLC with a majority of corporate characteristics, and viewed as a corporation for federal income tax purposes, may have membership interests that are virtually indistinguishable from common stock in a corporation. If so, the membership interest could be deemed a security on that basis. Even if an interest in an LLC is determined to be a security, one or more applicable exemptions may obviate registering the securities. Exemptions from the federal securities registration requirement may be available to a person selling membership interests to a small group of investors with whom there is a pre-existing relationship, sales to individuals with a substantial net worth (so-called *accredited investors*) and sales made to persons in only one state (an *intrastate offering*). The applicability of the federal securities law is a complex question and needs to be judged on a business-by-business basis. An explanation of the securities registration process is beyond the scope of this book, but its importance should not be overlooked.

In addition to the federal securities laws, each state has its own form of securities regulation, sometimes referred to as *blue-sky laws*. Some states have concluded that all membership interests in an LLC should be regarded as securities, other states have concluded that this issue can only be determined on a case-by-case basis and still other states have yet to consider the issue. If you are seeking to raise money for your LLC from a number of potential investors by the sale of membership interests, consult your attorney.

### Planning Tip 74

Unless an exemption applies to your LLC, properly register LLC membership interests that are determined to be securities with the Securities and Exchange Commission before soliciting to investors.

### Planning Tip 75

For information about possible exemptions from the securities registration process, consult your attorney.

### Planning Tip 76

Also consider the applicability of a state's blue-sky law to your LLC with your attorney if you intend to sell membership interests in your business.

### Planning Tip 77

Similar to the federal securities law, most states' blue-sky laws have exemptions from otherwise applicable registration requirements. For example, a state may exempt from registration an LLC that seeks to sell membership interests if

- the number of members of the LLC will not exceed 35,

- the seller believes the prospective members are purchasing interests for investment purposes only or
- the sale of membership interests is not made through a general solicitation. Consider these and other exemptions with your attorney.

### Entrepreneurs in Action

*Example 1.* John Smith needs to raise approximately $500,000 for his new restaurant business, which he has recently formed as an LLC. Over the years, he has invested approximately $50,000 of his own money with a group of ten wealthy individuals in his town. Each of these individuals has a minimum net worth in excess of $5 million. John calls each of the ten individuals and asks if they would like to invest in his business. They all say yes, and John sells them each a membership interest for $50,000. Because of John's prior relationship with these investors, their substantial net worth and the passive role they will play in the business, John's sale of membership interests in his LLC to these individuals may not constitute the sale of securities and, if it does, the sale should not require registration with the SEC because of applicable exemptions.

*Example 2.* The same situation as above but John's wealthiest acquaintance, who has a net worth of only $100,000, isn't interested in investing in John's business. John decides to send a blanket form letter to several hundred people whose names appear on a mailing list he purchased. Three individuals agree to invest money, but on the condition that they are given jobs in the business. Because of John's "unfocused" solicitation to many potential investors, his offering to sell ownership interests in his LLC probably requires appropriate registration with the SEC and, perhaps, his state's securities department as well.

# Creditors of Members

Most LLC acts provide that members of LLCs have no legal interest in specific property owned by the business. As a consequence, a creditor of any LLC member is precluded from asserting any rights against the LLC property directly. LLC acts generally allow a judgment creditor to obtain a charging order from an appropriate court. This can force the LLC to satisfy the creditor's claim out of distributions that would otherwise be made to the member. As we will see in Chapter 7, however, this remedy may not be very satisfactory, and the interests of the LLC and its members can often be well protected from harassing creditors.

# CHAPTER 6

# Creative Uses of LLCs

I can almost hear some of you grumble. "These LLCs sure sound great. Too bad my business is different. An LLC would never work in my situation!" Wanna bet? Although LLCs work beautifully for most common types of business operations, they also work well for some of the most complex and esoteric types of businesses and business organizations. In fact, not only do LLCs work well, in many cases they represent a substantial improvement over other business forms or techniques. In this chapter, we consider some creative planning opportunities that are now available to businesses and entrepreneurs thanks to the existence of LLCs.

## Joint Ventures

It is not uncommon for two or more existing businesses to collaborate with each other to pursue an opportunity. There are usually two principal reasons for joint venturing: money and liability.

Many joint ventures are formed because the cost of pursuing an opportunity is simply prohibitive for one business to undertake independently. If two or three or more businesses each dip into their savings or available credit, however, their respective costs may now be affordable. At the same time, new opportunities often pose new risks. The risk could arise from any number of factors: a potential for personal injury claims, a potential claim for patent infringements or a potential claim for hazardous waste cleanup, to name but a few examples.

An LLC now offers an ideal vehicle for joint venturers to combine their forces and pursue a potentially lucrative opportunity with a minimum degree of risk. With respect to potential liability claims, an LLC offers limited liability protection to its members. Accordingly, two successful businesses, for example, could take a chance on a new venture together without concern that their established businesses will be at risk.

An LLC's partnership tax treatment can also be used to allocate the cash, tax and other financial aspects of the business in a way that maximizes the benefits to each joint venturer. This attractive flexibility is often unavailable in corporations. Moreover, LLCs are able to pass through economic benefits to members without being taxed at the business level. Corporations, on the other hand, are often only able to distribute such benefits by declaring taxable dividends. In short, LLCs seem to be a substantial improvement upon the corporation form for joint venturers.

### Entrepreneurs in Action

*Example 1.* John Smith has operated a restaurant as a corporation for many years. In the past year, he has developed a delicious new snack, fat-free apple pie. He wants to start manufacturing pies for sale and distribution across the country. He can't, however, afford to do so on his own. He approaches a local cake manufacturer who has been interested in expanding its line to include pies, but hasn't yet found a recipe it likes. After sampling John's pies, the company management decides this is what they've been looking for. The two parties set up a new corporation to progress the concept.

*Analysis.* Although a new corporation provides the parties with limited liability protection for any claims or obligations that the new business incurs, the corporation incurs an entity level tax and the distributions to the two shareholders are taxed again (the double-level tax). They ask their accountants about electing S corporation status but learn, because its stock is, in turn, held by two corporations, they can't qualify. They must continue paying the double-level tax.

*Example 2.* Same example as above, but instead of setting up a corporation the parties form an LLC.

*Analysis.* As with a corporation, the LLC will provide its members with limited liability protection, so the assets of their respective original businesses are safe. Because of its pass-through tax treatment, however, distributions to the members are taxed only once. Also, the LLC's flexibility permits the members to make special allocations on the use of any losses the business incurs, which can be used by the members. By contrast, corporations cannot make such special allocations, and the losses can only be used at the corporate level, not be passed through for use by its shareholders.

## Entrepreneurial Financing Vehicles

Entrepreneurs will also find LLCs useful for raising capital. In the past, entrepreneurs have often struggled to raise money for a new business: General partnerships could not provide outside investors with the limited liability protection they might desire; investors who purchased limited partnerships units could not play any meaningful role in the management of the business; S corporations could not confer priority or preferred status on outside investors because of the one class of stock limitation; and C corporations incurred the double level of tax.

LLCs can be structured to surmount each of these obstacles. Outside investors can, as members, have the following benefits:

- Limited liability protection
- A role in the management of the business that the parties agree is appropriate without risk of losing their limited liability protection
- Priority cash flows and special allocations of tax benefits
- Avoiding the double level of tax

In short, an entrepreneur can use an LLC to address both economic and control issues.

### Planning Tip 78

Consider structuring your LLC so that the entrepreneur, as the manager, can retain sufficient control of day-to-day business decisions while providing outside investors with economic incentives and certain management controls.

### Entrepreneurs in Action

John needs to raise $500,000 to set up a new restaurant business. He first seeks to attract partners, but potential investors are concerned about their liability exposure. He next solicits the investors about their interest in limited partnership units. This time, they are concerned about not being involved in managing the business as limited partners. He considers C corporations, but the investors wish to avoid the double level of tax, and the S corporation won't work because some of the investors are corporations or hold their money in trust. Exacerbated, John finally suggests using an LLC. To his pleasant surprise, they are delighted with the limited liability protection, pass-through tax treatment, lack of restrictions on membership and the ability to participate in the management of the business that the LLC offers. All the investors agree to buy membership interests in John's LLC, and he now has the capital he needs to proceed with his business!

## Facilitating International Transactions

LLCs should prove valuable for promoting international transactions. Aside from its overall attractiveness, LLCs, unlike S corporations, can be owned, in whole or in part, by foreigners and foreign businesses. This feature should encourage the use of foreign capital when U.S. sources of capital lack interest or available funds for a particular business opportunity.

LLCs may also have significant tax saving advantages over S corporations when operating abroad. For example, many foreign countries have historically treated S corporations as taxable business entities, ignoring its pass-through tax status otherwise conferred under U.S. law. In effect, S corporations operating abroad are often forced to pay the double level of tax as if they were C corporations. Many of these same countries, however, have their own entities that are similar to LLCs and are taxed on a pass-through basis. Although little precedent is available on this issue, logic suggests that an LLC properly formed within the United States will be treated analogously to its foreign counterpart—and thus secure pass-through tax treatment abroad.

### Planning Tip 79

Use your LLC to develop opportunities abroad!

### Entrepreneurs in Action

John meets an old friend from college for dinner one night and they discuss John's planned restaurant business. The friend, a Canadian citizen, is excited and wants to invest with John. If they set up a corporation, it will be ineligible for S corporation status, because of the friend's citizenship, and so will incur a double level of tax as a regular corporation. As an alternative, they can set up an LLC and have the benefits of pass-through taxation because LLCs do not restrict foreigners from holding membership interests.

## High Technology Ventures

Many of the reasons that make an LLC attractive for joint ventures also make it an attractive choice for high technology ventures. To the extent that the venturers are concerned about their liability exposure—for example, by the malfunction of their technology—the LLC's limited liability feature is ideal. If the product takes off, the LLC form allows the venturers to avoid the entity-level tax otherwise extracted from a C corporation. The LLC's flexibility further allows the venturers to allocate their profits, losses, distributions, management rights and capital contribution requirements freely. The ability of a highly talented individual to contribute his or her services in exchange for a membership interest in the LLC without recognizing taxable income will also help ensure the successful use of LLCs in high technology venturers.

### Entrepreneurs in Action

John Smith's oldest son, John, Jr., is a scientific genius. After several years of experimentation, he has developed a new wireless beeper that is more efficient than other existing beepers. John, Jr., who has no money, approaches a manufacturer. They agree to set up an LLC together. John, Jr., contributes his technology and services for a 40 percent membership interest; the manufacturer contributes capital for a 60 percent interest. The manufacturer likes the limited liability protection; John, Jr., is happy that he can contribute his technology and services for a membership interest on a tax-free basis. He is advised that if he were making this contribution in exchange for stock in a corporation, he would likely be required to pay tax.

## Business Reorganizations

Although it is beyond the scope of this book to examine the treatment of LLCs in bankruptcy, LLCs can confer benefits on their members in both good times and bad. First, an LLC's pass-through tax treatment permits the special allocation of losses—and the ability to use such losses—by and to its members. As discussed in Chapter 8, this may result in greater tax benefits to LLC members than to corporate shareholders. Second, use of the LLC ensures that the members will have limited liability protection and should not be exposed to creditor claims, in the event the reorganization is unsuccessful. Finally, as previously noted, it is expected that LLCs will qualify to seek such relief under the Bankruptcy Code. Available relief, including the automatic stay of prepetition claims by creditors, can be helpful to any business and its owners during a financial crisis.

### Planning Tip 80

Consider what should happen upon (heaven forbid!) the bankruptcy of your business or one of its owners and include an appropriate provision in your operating agreement. Consider addressing such subjects as the following:

- Whether the bankruptcy of one member should dissolve the LLC
- Whether a bankrupt member's interest may be assignable to another party, either in whole or in part
- Whether the old guard management of the LLC should be replaced by new management upon the filing of a petition

## Real Estate Investments

LLCs should prove attractive to investors in real estate who seek some management role in the business, limited liability and the opportunity to benefit from the favorable tax treatment of certain nonrecourse debt. Here's why.

The general partnership form has historically been unattractive to real estate investors because partners lack limited liability protection. Limited partnerships, perhaps the most commonly used business form in real estate transactions, are often unsuitable because they preclude limited partners from actively participating in the management of the business or risk losing their limited liability protection. S corporations also are unpopular because their shareholders can only use tax losses up to the limit of their capital contributions in the business plus any loans they have personally made or guaranteed. Moreover, the use of S corporations by real estate developers is not always attractive because the one class of stock requirement makes it difficult or impossible to establish different allocations among investors. Also, the S status can be inadvertently terminated by an investor's transfer of his or her ownership interest to a shareholder who does not meet the stringent S corporation eligibility requirements. Although the IRS sometimes issues waivers, the process typically requires securing a favorable private letter ruling, which can be costly and time consuming.

The hybrid nature of the LLC allows it to provide the best of these features to real estate investors and avoid the worst. Specifically, real estate investors using an LLC could secure limited liability protection, the opportunity to participate actively in the management of the LLC without losing their limited liability protection, and, because of the tax treatment of partnerships, the use of certain nonrecourse debt (i.e., for which they have no personal liability) to create recognizable tax losses—even if such losses exceed the investor's capital contributions. Individuals involved in the rental of real estate are familiar with the limitations of tax losses imposed by the passive-loss rules of the Internal Revenue Code (see Chapter 8). Like other business forms, it is expected that LLCs involved in the rental of real estate will ordinarily be deemed to be engaged in a passive activity except for those professional real estate businesses that may be qualified for an exemption.

### Planning Tip 81

Consider the applicability of the passive-loss tax rules to your real estate deal.

### Planning Tip 82

Because it has no eligibility requirements for membership, you can use an LLC to attract different investors, with different objectives, to pursue profitable real estate transactions.

## Professional Service Firms

LLCs and limited liability partnerships (LLPs) may be especially useful for professional service firms. Many LLC acts even expressly authorize the establishment of professional service LLCs. An LLP is a new form of partnership with limited liability features. Because of its importance, this subject is discussed in more detail in Chapter 11. Evidence of its usefulness includes the fact that each of the Big 6 accounting firms has already converted to an LLP, as have many large and prominent law firms. Why have so many professional service firms switched to LLCs and LLPs? The same reasons other businesses are doing so: limited liability protection, pass-through tax treatment and management flexibility.

By practicing in an LLC or LLP firm, a professional can secure limited liability protection against all claims except those arising from the professional's own negligence or the negligence of another whom the professional supervised. In this way, the professional can protect personal assets from claims arising out of contractual obligations, the malpractice of one or more of the professional's partners or any other claim unrelated to rendering professional services. Properly structured, the LLC or LLP should also provide the pass-through partnership tax treatment and management flexibility typically desired by professionals. Most states, of course, heavily regulate the practice of lawyers, accountants and other professionals. A few states, including California and Rhode Island, even expressly prohibit professionals from operating as LLCs. Accordingly, such individuals should be careful to consider the acceptability of these forms in their jurisdictions.

An important question for many professionals is whether they can use the *cash method* of accounting or whether they will be required to use the *accrual method.* The issue can be critical because many professionals often carry significant receivables, which sometimes go uncollected. To be forced to pay tax on receivables before their actual collection could prove a hardship. Fortunately, initial private letter rulings from the IRS suggest that the cash method can be used by professionals operating in LLCs or LLPs.

### Planning Tip 83

Remember, an LLC, LLP or any other business form does NOT limit a professional's liability for his or her own malpractice. As a professional, prepare your safety net against such claims with sufficient insurance coverage.

### Planning Tip 84

Discuss your use of the cash or accrual accounting method with your tax adviser when forming your LLC.

## Investment Groups

LLCs can be an attractive vehicle for investors who wish to pool their resources as part of their investment strategy. Investors may be able to take advantage of lucrative opportunities as part of a group that they could otherwise not pursue with only their individual resources. An LLC's flexibility allows greater involvement by investors in selecting investment strategies than do, for example, mutual funds, which are also subject to double-level taxation. Members are free to agree on contribution levels, investment strategies and standards for withdrawing capital. Investors with similar objectives may even choose to form an LLC and then hire a manager to service their collective portfolio, which may prove easier than if each tried to manage his or her own individual investments. The members can agree in advance on the selection of a qualified money manager or spell out in the LLC's operating agreement what the minimum level of education and experience must be and then designate one or a group of members to locate an acceptable candidate. The manager may, but need not be, a member of the LLC as well.

### Planning Tip 85

Investor groups should consider whether their LLC's operating agreement should specify each member's capital contribution, each member's interest in the LLC's profits and losses, each member's interest in the LLC's cash flow and each member's right to capital upon liquidation.

### Entrepreneurs in Action

John Smith approaches one of his best friends, Tom Black, to see whether Tom is interested in investing in a new restaurant venture. Tom is excited about the marketing concept and surveys suggesting it will be a huge success. Unfortunately, Tom does not have enough of his own money to make the necessary investment. After some discussion, they agree that Tom can form a new LLC, of which he is the exclusive manager. Tom will approach several members of his family who have money to invest and will sell them membership interests in his LLC; under the operating agreement, these investors will have no management role. John is happy because he has raised necessary capital. Tom is happy because he can pursue an attractive investment opportunity, by pooling money from various sources. Tom's family is happy because they too can share in the same good opportunity without having to spend time on managing their investment. They can delegate this responsibility to Tom and, ultimately, John, and can now just sit back and collect their distribution checks.

## Oil and Gas

An LLC may be appealing for use in the oil and gas business. The exploration and production of oil and gas is fraught with hazards and risk. Fires, blow-outs, explosions and poisonous gas are some of the potential dangers faced in this business. LLCs could be a useful new tool by which investors limit their liability if any one of these or similar events occurs. Not only could an investor limit his or her personal liability but, by establishing multiple LLCs for different hazardous properties, investors could also limit liability on a project-by-project basis, further enhancing the protection available for their overall business interests. In addition, the tax code authorizes the use of special deductions for the oil and gas industry, such as one based on the depletion of a producing property. Historically, the industry has found it desirable to allocate these deductions to the individual investors contributing the producing property to the business. As discussed above, LLCs can easily be structured to allocate such deductions specifically to their members who contribute producing property and provide different deductions to members who, for example, contribute only cash.

### Planning Tip 86

To help make sure that special allocations of deductions meet the substantial economic effect test under the tax code (discussed in Chapter 8), consider creating different classes of membership interests for your LLC with different distribution rights.

### Entrepreneurs in Action

Aside from being a successful restaurateur, John Smith has invested in the oil business over the years. He learns from an acquaintance of a new opportunity to invest in an offshore site in the North Sea. Because of the rough water, high winds and other inherent dangers in drilling for oil, he is concerned about exposing his personal and other business assets to liability claims in the event of disaster. After learning that five new LLCs have been organized to drill on five separately identified sites, John decides to invest because his assets are protected and his liability limited to his investments on a site-by-site basis.

# CHAPTER 7

# Using Your LLC To Plan Your Estate

Owners of family and closely held businesses often spend an enormous amount of time, money and emotion on the transfer of ownership and control of their business to their successors, typically children and grandchildren. The process is full of difficulties and, unfortunately, such businesses rarely make it to the second or third generation of ownership. A wide variety of factors are responsible for this breakdown, including the following:

- A senior generation owner's reluctance to relinquish control of the business to his or her successor
- Parental confusion about the fairest way to treat their children who are active in the business and their children who are not
- The high price of keeping a business extracted by federal and state governments in the form of estate and gift taxes
- Family disputes
- Marital discord

Most business owners struggle with their attorneys and accountants to address these and other concerns. Complex arrangements that permit an owner to retain management control over a business while relinquishing the ownership interest have been devised. Others have been conceived to reduce taxes, resolve disputes, etc., etc., etc. Many of these arrangements are complex and unwieldy. Their success is often difficult to measure.

The selection of the most suitable business form for your situation is not a panacea to the difficult problems associated with the transfer of your business. That would be expecting too much. Instead the requirements for a smooth transfer are communication, planning, consensus building, agreement and, ultimately, a commitment to follow up the agreement with action. If the people involved are blessed with the necessary wisdom, demeanor and stamina to pursue this process, then, and only then, can the tools available to lawyers and accountants make a difference.

Make no mistake, though! The LLC is one of the newest and most exciting tools now available to business succession planners. I believe its qualities allow it to easily outperform its counterparts—general and limited partnerships and corporations—in helping to get the business transfer job done. The LLC in the hands of a capable business owner and his advisers offers unique planning opportunities that may help improve the likelihood of your creating a workable transfer plan. This chapter will help show you how!

### Planning Tip 87

Consider with your attorney how using an LLC can facilitate your estate planning.

## LLCs Can Help Solve the Succession Problem

As noted above, some of the most difficult issues in the estate planning process concern control. Everybody seems to want it! Parents, children, spouses, in-laws—the list goes on. In addition to control, everybody wants a fair share of the income, profits and value of the business. Although it's not always possible to satisfy these competing demands, LLCs can help.

First, as we learned in preceding chapters, an LLC's organizational documents can be prepared to fit the particular objectives of its members. Profits can be allocated in any number of ways. So, too, can losses. The management of a business can also be structured in almost any manner that satisfies the interests of its members; there is no limit to the number of ownership and management classes that can be created.

An LLC's extraordinary flexibility can be used to help resolve the problems caused by competing demands commonly encountered in the business succession process. Indeed, the imagination and creativity of the succession planner may be the most imposing limit to the use of an LLC to address such problems. Let's see how an LLC can help facilitate a succession plan by examining the common problem faced by a business owner who wants to transfer all or part of the business to reduce transfer taxes yet retain management control of the operation.

## A Sample Solution to the Succession Problem

Business owners are regularly advised to start transferring their business to their children as early as possible in order to minimize the high cost of estate and gift taxes. Given that tax rates can often reach 60 percent of an owner's estate, the advice is often sound. In many cases, the earlier the transfer of ownership is made, the greater the amount of tax that can be avoided. How? Consider the case of a parent who has a business worth $1 today and expected to be worth $2 next year. If the parent retains ownership of the business and dies next year, he or she will owe $1.20 in tax (assuming a 60 percent tax rate), leaving the net estate with $.80. If, however, the parent transfers the business to the children today, say in exchange for $1 in cash, only $.60 of estate tax on the $1 would be due on the parent's death, leaving the net estate with $.40. The children not only receive the $.40, but have put the $1 in appreciation in their pocket and, so, exempt from tax.

Although you need not be a math whiz to understand why transferring a business that is increasing (or appreciating) in value to your heirs as soon as possible will save money, many business owners are reluctant to do so. Why? A primary reason is the owner's reluctance to relinquish control of the business. LLCs to the rescue!

An LLC can be structured so that the younger generation benefits from the appreciation in value of the business while the senior generation retains all or part of the management control. Various techniques can accomplish this purpose, such as using two classes of membership interests, one with management rights and the other without. The children get the latter and the parent gets the former. Alternatively, the parent can relinquish all of his or her ownership interest in an LLC but require the children, as a condition of becoming members, to sign an operating agreement that appoints the parent as manager of the business for life (or other event which the parent chooses).

### Entrepreneurs in Action

Having now reached the point in his life where he wants to slow down, John Smith considers his estate planning situation. His restaurant business has flourished over the years and shows no signs of letting up. "How," John asks his adviser, "can I transfer all or part of my ownership interest to my three children yet retain a certain level of control over business decisions?"

"Easy," answers John's attorney. "Start transferring ownership interests in your LLC to your children. Make the kids sign an operating agreement that names you as the exclusive manager. If the value of the business continues to increase, the benefit will go to your children and will escape gift or estate tax. As the manager, you retain exclusive control over business decisions. When you want, you can amend the operating agreement to add one or more of your children as co-managers or you can completely resign."

Although John asks for more details, he is beginning to like the sound of this transfer plan.

## LLCs Can Be Used To Help Treat Children Equitably

What can a parent do to treat his or her children fairly in an estate plan when one child is active in the business, the other children are not and the bulk of the parent's wealth is locked-up in the business? Easy. Use an LLC!

A parent in this situation struggles with the apparent conflict created by wishing to treat all of the children equally. Nevertheless, the parent doesn't want to leave the child who is active in the business in an intolerable situation where his or her decisions are secondguessed by siblings who know little, if anything, about the business. The same flexibility that permits a parent to retain management control also permits that parent to allocate the same control to the active child. For example, the parent could give all the children equal membership interests in an LLC but only the active child would receive an ownership interest with management rights. Alternatively, the parent could appoint the active child as the exclusive manager of the business, subject to being terminated in only narrowly defined events. Other possibilities could work too, but you get the idea.

### Entrepreneurs in Action

In designing his estate plan, John is not sure how to treat his three children. John, Jr., left the high tech beeper business many years ago and has been working diligently in the restaurant business. His talent and effort have help build the operations into one of the largest privately owned chains in the state. John's other children, Jimmy and Jane, have gone in separate directions. Although John wants to treat his three children fairly, he doesn't want John, Jr., to have his hands tied by siblings unfamiliar with the business. John's lawyer suggests transferring equal membership interests in the LLC to each child, but naming John, Jr., as exclusive manager and increasing his salary to reflect added job responsibilities. This way, all the children receive equal distributions of income and profit in their capacity as owners, but John, Jr. has control of the business plus additional compensation for the services he renders on behalf of the business.

# LLCs Can Be Gifted and Sold

The techniques used by attorneys and accountants to transfer ownership of a business are, ultimately, variations of a simple gift from a donor to a donee or a sale from a seller to a buyer. For example, the most commonly used estate planning technique is for an individual to make outright gifts of $10,000 or less in cash or equivalents to his or her heirs, since, under the Internal Revenue Code, such gifts are not taxable. Another common technique is a redemption of stock, which is really a form of stock sale from a shareholder to a corporation. An annuity is a sale of stock from a shareholder to a third party. Such strange-sounding estate planning techniques as GRATS, GRITS, CRATS and CRUTS all are esoteric forms of sales or gifts.

There does not appear to be any reason why most, if not all, of these traditional transfer techniques cannot be used to transfer LLC membership interests. Indeed, because of available management control provisions, a donor or seller may be more inclined to transfer a membership interest in an LLC, knowing that control can be effectively retained without ownership. This may be particularly true when transfers are made to young children. Let's consider one example.

A transfer of stock in a corporation can produce premature financial benefits to a child. For example, a child with even one share of stock may be entitled to receive a substantial dividend. As more and more shares are transferred to the child on a regular basis, the size of the dividends may continue to grow. A parent wishes to continue transferring stock to reduce estate taxes, but is concerned that the dividends will reduce the child's incentives to develop a healthy work ethic. In many cases, the parent can't arbitrarily cut off dividends, even if all shareholders are also cut off, because the corporation could then be subject to a retained earnings tax on the money it should have distributed, but didn't. LLCs, by contrast, are not subject to the retained earnings tax and, so, could retain income in the business without penalty. Moreover, because LLCs can allocate income to some members and not others, it should be easy to draft an operating agreement that allocates business income to the parents but not the children. The agreement may even specify that when children reach a certain age or contribute to the business in certain positive ways, they would get specified levels of distributions, in effect, creating different classes of ownership interests for different children.

Finally, many parents have been disappointed with the results of giving each of their children particular business assets because it is commonplace for the value of one or more of such assets to increase while that of other assets decreases, often for reasons wholly unrelated to the efforts of the children. LLCs can be used to consolidate a parent's assets and, by transferring membership interests (with or without management rights) to children, the children should share more fairly in the future growth of all assets.

### Planning Tip 88

Consider consolidating your assets (including multiple businesses) in an LLC to minimize management, administrative and other costs.

### Entrepreneurs in Action

John Smith acquired undeveloped land many years ago. Instead of developing the land as originally contemplated, he ignored it, focusing instead on his restaurant business. Now, the land is ripe for development and a local mall developer is eager to acquire the property.

As part of his estate plans, John could, of course, divide the property in equal portions and give these portions outright to his children. He is concerned, however, that this option may impede the orderly sale of the property to a qualified developer at the highest possible price. His solution? An LLC! Instead of making outright gifts of divided parcels, John could form an LLC and contribute the property to it. He could transfer the entire ownership of the LLC to his children, who would be the only members in the business. At the same time, John could require the children to sign an operating agreement that appoints him as manager of the LLC. As manager, he could take steps to maximize the sale price for the undivided property. Once sold, the LLC could distribute its assets—the proceeds from the sale—to its members (John's children) according to the allocation provisions John selected when forming the LLC!

### Planning Tip 89

Consider drafting your family LLC's operating agreement to give one or both parents the exclusive right to manage the business and determine whether any distributions should be made. Also consider including in the agreement a provision that denies nonmanager members (i.e., the children) the right to force a liquidation of the LLC.


## The Value of an LLC Interest Is Subject to Discounts

A key element of any estate plan involving a family or closely held business is valuation. The lower the value of a business, the easier it is to transfer because less tax needs to be paid. Accordingly, the subject of fixing business value receives a lot of attention. The traditional measure of value is the price at which the business would change hands between a willing buyer and a willing seller, neither being forced to buy or sell and both understanding the relevant facts. Notwithstanding the sensibleness of this standard, fixing value remains impossible to do accurately if no actual sale to a third party occurs or if ownership interests of the business don't freely trade on a public market. Nevertheless, the attempt must be made and a number of formulas have been developed over the years to help accomplish this task.

Valuation analysis has historically recognized that certain reductions, or discounts, on the value of a business are permissible. These discounts, which have saved business owners substantial sums, are largely based on the premise that all ownership interests in a business cannot always be treated equally. In other words, a share of stock that one person owns may have a different value than a share owned by someone else. How can that be? The free market sets the price and everyone buys or sells at the market price. Right? Not always!

In the real world, certain ownership interests in a business are more desirable than others because of the control or the comparative ease with which they can be transferred. In recognition of these factors, the IRS has acknowledged that the value of certain ownership interests in businesses should be reduced, or discounted, in appropriate circumstances. It is now common for certain ownership interests in business to be discounted for lack of marketability and minority interest. For example, if sufficient restrictions in an LLC's organizational documents limit a member's right to transfer his or her ownership interest, a discount for lack of marketability should be applicable. All else being equal, an ownership interest that is not freely transferable is worth less than one that is. Similarly, a minority interest discount recognizes the often unenviable status of being a minority owner: They are at the mercy of the majority owners unless the company's organizational documents otherwise confer management control on the minority owner. These discounts should all continue to apply when valuing the interests of LLC members and may serve to reduce the value of a gift or sale of an interest in an LLC.

Although each situation needs to be considered on its own merits, traditional (combined) discounts for lack of control and lack of marketability in other business forms may range from 20 percent to 40 percent. Equivalent discounts are expected to be recognized in analogous situations involving LLCs. Even larger discounts may be possible for LLCs than for other business forms if a member is able to cause a dissolution of the business upon death or voluntary withdrawal. The lack of stability may make an LLC's value less than that of a similar business operated in a more stable form. Of course, as discussed in Chapter 10, techniques are available to increase stability by helping to ensure the likelihood of the business continuing.

While a minority interest in an LLC may be subject to a discount, it may also be possible for certain members who control an LLC to have the value of their interest increased by the imposition of a control premium by the IRS. Given the management options in an LLC, be alert to this potential problem. For example, a membership interest of 10 percent held by a manager is probably worth more than a membership interest held by a nonmanager member.

### Planning Tip 90

Consider the use of traditional discounts when valuing your LLC.

### Planning Tip 91

If your LLC will likely continue operations after an event of dissolution, consider valuing a distribution to a withdrawing member on the assumption that the business will continue (as opposed to its being liquidated).

### Planning Tip 92

Be alert to the possible imposition of a control premium on the value of controlling interests in your LLC.

## LLCs Can Be Used To Help Resolve Family Disputes

The best laid business transfer plans often run amuck because of unanticipated conflict between family members. An LLC can be used to help resolve these often inevitable disputes with a minimum of bloodshed. All of the established mechanisms to resolve disputes can be incorporated for use in LLCs. For example, an LLC's operating agreement can provide for a dispute between members to be resolved by majority vote, by a family leader, by an outsider, by an arbitrator, by a mediator or by any other appropriate mechanism. The agreement can even establish the ground rules for resolving the dispute—time frames, rules of evidence, the binding or nonbinding nature of a decision maker's authority—in any manner to which the members agree.

### Entrepreneurs in Action

John Smith would like his three children to inherit the restaurant empire he has amassed over the years. After preparing an appropriate transfer plan that minimizes the tax consequences of the transfer, he has only one concern left. His children, Jane and John, Jr., are both married and, although they get along, their spouses don't. Although Jimmy isn't married yet, he never seems to have enough money and his constant requests for more have caused resentment among his siblings and their spouses. In spite of the substantial salary John pays him, it never seems like enough money to Jimmy. John is concerned that his transfer plan is a ticking time bomb. He is convinced that the moment he dies, his children will be in court, suing each other over something silly. What can John do to reduce the possibility of a damaging family conflict? Use an LLC!

John could transfer all of the membership interest in his restaurant business to his three children, along with all, part or none of the management control, subject to an operating agreement. The agreement could include an appropriate dispute resolution mechanism or even a combination of mechanisms. For example, if Jim unilaterally seeks to increase his own salary, Jane and John, Jr., could use the mechanism their father had established in the operating agreement (say the appointment of an arbitrator) to challenge the salary increase. Although the children may not always like the results, such dispute resolution mechanisms are much cheaper and far less bloody then the alternative—litigation!

### Planning Tip 93

Include a dispute resolution mechanism in your operating agreement.

### Planning Tip 94

Consider including a provision in your operating agreement that requires the losing member in a dispute to pay attorneys' fees. Many foreign countries find this requirement promotes early settlements and helps reduce the assertion of frivolous claims.

## LLCs Can Limit Children's Access to Assets

Parents may wish to transfer valuable assets to their children as part of their estate plan but, at the same time, are concerned that their children are too young or too inactive to manage their new wealth. LLCs can solve the problem.

The parents can put their valuable assets into an LLC and then gift or sell membership interests in the business to their children. The LLC's operating agreement can be drafted to provide that the class of member made up of the children shall not have any right to require a distribution of LLC assets without the consent of the parent-manager (or prior to dissolution). The parent-manager also can provide in the operating agreement that he or she has exclusive control over distribution of the LLC's cash. The parent-manager thereby retains complete discretion about whether to distribute cash to the children, and, if so, how much and to whom, or, alternatively, whether the cash should be reinvested in the business.

### Planning Tip 95

Use an LLC to strategically transfer your assets to your children while retaining a desired level of control.

## LLCs Can Protect Owners in the Event of Divorce

One of the most common concerns of a business owner who is transferring ownership interests in his or her business to a child is what would happen to the interest in the event of a child's divorce? Would the exspouse have a right to a portion of the ownership interest? What about maintaining or securing voting influence? These and related issues can cause owners many a sleepless night. An LLC can now be used to help reduce or even eliminate these concerns.

One strategy is to address the consequences of divorce in the operating agreement. An appropriate provision could state that the LLC (or family member) could elect to purchase any membership interest that is held by the exspouse or that could be awarded to an exspouse pursuant to a dissolution agreement or divorce decree. In effect, the operating agreement functions much as a traditional buy-sell agreement would in the same circumstance.

### Planning Tip 96

Use your operating agreement in conjunction with a prenuptial agreement to specify the consequences of a spouse's divorce from a member.

### Planning Tip 97

Specify in your operating agreement the procedure to be followed if a decision is made to acquire the exspouse's interest, including, for example, how the price for the interest will be established, when it must be paid and when the decision to buy out the exspouse must be made.

## LLCs Can Provide Protection from Creditors

A common concern shared by parents who are transferring assets to their children is how these assets can be protected against the possible claims of their children's creditors in the future. By restricting the free transferability of ownership interests (which can help ensure favorable partnership tax treatment), LLCs can reduce the need for such concern. As we learned in Chapter 4, the rule is well established in most states that creditors of an LLC member cannot satisfy their claims by seizing property of the LLC. Instead, creditors are usually only able to secure a *charging order* against the member's LLC interest. A charging order ordinarily only gives a creditor the status of an assignee of the membership interest and not of a member. The result? The creditor will neither acquire a governance interest in the business and will be unable to impair the members' managerial control over the business, nor will he or she be able to force a distribution of cash or other property to satisfy the claim.

**Planning Tip 98**

Help shelter your children's assets from creditors by using an LLC.

**Entrepreneurs in Action**

John Smith has given a one-third membership interest in his LLC to his son, Jimmy. Jimmy is a spendthrift and soon finds himself near bankruptcy, with a number of creditors seeking to be repaid. Although the creditors may be able to seize most of Jimmy's property, they can't touch his LLC membership interest. Instead, they could secure a charging order, entitling them to the distributions Jimmy would otherwise receive from the business. John Smith could, however, retain the LLC's earnings in the business if he has legitimate business reasons. Worse still for the hapless creditor, he may be forced to pay income tax on Jimmy's share of the LLC income, even if no distributions are made to pay the tax. As a result of these legal consequences, it should be possible for Jimmy to work out an advantageous settlement with his creditors.

# LLCs Can Facilitate Insurance Planning

A common estate planning technique in recent years involves the use of irrevocable life insurance trusts (ILIT). For example, a father concerned about transferring wealth to his children can set up an ILIT, name the children as beneficiaries of the trust and fund the trust with an insurance policy that the parent pays for by gifting the requisite premiums to the children. Because the parent has relinquished all control over the cash used for the premium and never had control over the policy (because of the terms of the trust), the insurance proceeds payable on his death are *not* part of the estate and, so, are not reduced by otherwise applicable estate taxes. This neat trick has only one drawback. Applicable law requires the ILIT to be irrevocable. In other words, it can't be changed for any reason whatsoever—even unforeseen circumstances such as the death or divorce of a child that might otherwise prompt a reasonable parent to seek a change.

LLCs may now provide an attractive alternative to ILITs. Let's consider the case of another parent, this time a mother. Instead of forming an irrevocable trust, she forms an LLC and contributes cash that is used to purchase an insurance policy on her life. The parent could keep a small membership interest or could even keep nothing. The children would own all or most of the LLC. The parent could name herself as manager of the LLC for any period of time, including for her life, and her appointment would be recognized in the LLC's operating agreement. The parent could even be authorized to amend the LLC's organizational documents or terminate its existence.

Like an ILIT, such an LLC may be able to provide tax-free insurance benefits upon the parent's death to the children because the proceeds would be distributed to the children who own most or all of the LLC. Unlike the ILIT, however, the LLC is not irrevocable but rather is extremely flexible. The parent can change any aspect of the structure she chooses to in light of changing circumstances, including accessing the policy's cash value and changing the beneficiaries or their share of the death benefits. Because of complex applicable estate tax rules, you should be careful to consider this planning opportunity in conjunction with your advisers.

### Planning Tip 99

Consider using an LLC to hold your insurance instead of an irrevocable life insurance trust.

## LLCs Can Easily Respond to a Changing Environment

Families change. So do laws, tax rates, the marketplace, the competition, etc. etc. etc. The families and businesses that are successful don't resist change. They embrace it! LLCs can prove a valuable tool for such achievers. The operating agreement of an LLC can be drafted with change in mind. Amendments to the agreement can be accomplished, if necessary. Centralized management can be ready to welcome change without having its hands tied by members who may be uninformed and unprepared or unwilling to take any action without substantial delay. LLCs can even be liquidated and dissolved if necessary, often without tax costs to the members. In short, the members of an LLC can use its flexibility to respond quickly and cheaply to an ever-changing environment.

## LLCs Can Outperform Family Partnerships

*Family limited partnerships* (FLPs) have received considerable acclaim over the years for their contribution to the estate planning process. Although the acclaim is well deserved, LLCs provide many of the same advantages as do FLPs plus some extras. For example, in an FLP, a general partner is personally liable for the debts and obligations of the business; in an LLC, all the members have limited liability. In an FLP, limited partners cannot materially participate in the management of the business without losing their limited liability protection; in an LLC, all members can (if desired) participate in the management. In an FLP, partnership obligations do not increase the basis of the limited partners' interests unless they personally guarantee the obligations; in an LLC, nonrecourse debt *can* increase the basis of the members' interests even without personal guarantees. In short, careful comparison between these two alternative forms suggests that the LLC may be the better way to go.

### Planning Tip 100

Consider using an LLC instead of a family limited partnership.

# Anti-Abuse Restrictions

The IRS has developed a variety of common law principles that enable it to recast certain transactions whose principal purpose is to secure a reduction in tax benefits in a manner inconsistent with the *intent* of the tax code. Some of these principles are commonly referred to by such names as *step transactions, substance over form transactions* and *sham transactions*. Because of the extraordinary planning opportunities presented by the use of LLCs, the IRS has taken a hard look at whether it should curb the use of family-owned LLCs for tax avoidance purposes. Initially, the IRS sought to extend its final version of the partnership anti-abuse regulations to include family LLCs that were formed to avoid or minimize estate or gift taxes. The regulation was criticized and the IRS, finally, decided to limit its rule to the avoidance of income but not estate or gift taxes. The federal tax rules in this area, for all forms of business, including LLCs, are complex and ever changing. The IRS can be expected to continually reassess its treatment of what it perceives to be tax planning strategies that are "too good to be true." Accordingly, when developing your estate planning strategy, especially if you want to use some of the aggressive techniques discussed in this chapter, do so with advice from qualified counsel.

# CHAPTER 8

# Beneficial Tax Treatment of LLCs

Few subjects are as important yet intimidating to business owners as is the topic of federal income taxation. The mere mention of such terms as basis, special allocations and passive-loss rules makes many a businessowner's head spin. As complex as this area may be, it should neither be feared nor ignored by business owners as much as my experience suggests it currently seems to be. Although no book can substitute for a careful analysis of the specific facts and circumstances facing your business, this chapter has been written to give you a broad overview of how LLC income is taxed so you can work with, and not just listen to, your tax adviser.

Because of the complexity of the Internal Revenue Code, many businesspeople (and even some of their advisers) believe that since S corporations and partnerships are both pass-through entities, they are taxed in the same way. In fact, however, there are significant differences. We will consider certain examples below. Many of these differences make partnership tax treatment preferable. These preferences can further enhance the desirability of using an LLC over an S corporation. Because of the many unique features found in each state's income tax laws, this chapter concentrates on how LLCs are treated under the federal income tax.

### Planning Tip 101

In addition to considering federal tax consequences, be careful to review with a knowledgeable adviser the applicable state income tax consequences of operating your business as an LLC.

# LLCs Are Generally Taxed as Partnerships

We learned in Chapter 1 that certain business entities, such as proprietorships, partnerships and S corporations, receive pass-through tax treatment under the federal income tax law while other business entities, most notably regular corporations, do not. In Chapter 2, we learned that LLCs also may be treated as pass-through entities and taxed as partnerships as long as they don't have three or more of the corporate characteristics considered by the IRS. As long as an LLC has fewer than three corporate characteristics, it should be subject to Subchapter K of the Internal Revenue Code and, so, generally taxed like a partnership. Because LLCs, unlike S corporations, can be owned by nonresident aliens, they are becoming an increasingly popular vehicle for U.S. citizens and foreigners to use when forming joint ventures. If the LLC is formed in a foreign country and qualifies to do business within the United States, the IRS will consider the law of that country to decide whether the entity is properly classified as a partnership or corporation for U.S. tax purposes. Because most business owners forming LLCs will desire partnership tax treatment, this chapter will assume such treatment is available. The analysis contained in this chapter is inapplicable in those relatively unusual cases where an LLC is taxed as a corporation.

### Planning Tip 102

If you establish a foreign LLC, be careful to evaluate the applicable foreign law. Also consider how your foreign source of income will be treated by the IRS

### Entrepreneurs in Action

John Smith would like to set up a restaurant business in a way that can confer a limited ownership interest on several key employees. His preference is to pay dividends to these employees if surplus cash is available. He considers the possible use of common stock and preferred stock to accomplish his objectives but is advised that it would preclude him from electing S corporation status because of the one class of stock requirement. He can, however, use an LLC to create what essentially amounts to *common* membership interests and *preferred* membership interests to accomplish his objectives.

## *Taxation at Membership Level Only*

Perhaps the most significant advantage of an LLC's being taxed like a partnership is that its income is taxed only once. The members are liable for any income tax due in their individual capacities. The business entity itself, however, is not taxed at all. By contrast, corporations pay a tax at the business entity level on income it earns and again on the shareholder level when dividends or other nondeductible distributions are received. Although S corporations are generally not taxed at the business entity level, we learned in Chapter 1 about the substantial eligibility requirements for this business form that many owners cannot meet.

### Entrepreneurs in Action

John and Mike are unclear about the savings they may realize by operating as an LLC and not as a regular corporation. They raise the question with their accountant, who prepares the following analysis:

*Smith Restaurants, LLC (Pass-through tax)*

| | | |
|---|---|---|
| Taxable income | = | $100,000 |
| − Tax to owner (rate = 30%) | = | 30,000 |
| Balance to owner | = | $ 70,000 |

*Smith Restaurants, Inc. (Double-level tax)*

| | | |
|---|---|---|
| Taxable income | = | $100,000 |
| − Corporate tax (rate = 30%) | = | 30,000 |
| Distribution to Owner | = | $ 70,000 |
| − Tax to owner (rate = 30%) | = | 21,000 |
| Balance to owner | = | $ 49,000 |

The accountant explains that John and Mike can realize a savings of $21,000 ($70,000 − $49,000) by operating their restaurant business as an LLC instead of as a regular corporation. They all agree it will be quite a savings.

## LLCs Report Income and Loss

An LLC is not a taxable entity under the Internal Revenue Code. Instead, it simply determines the amount and character of its income, losses, deductions and credits and then allocates such items (in the manner provided by law or by agreement of the members) to its members who, in turn, report their share of such items on their own individual tax returns. The LLC only files an information return with the IRS, in which it reports on the foregoing items but pays no tax. Let's turn, then, to some of the more important rules that govern how members of an LLC are taxed.

### No Tax on Formation of an LLC

Generally, no tax is due when members contribute assets to form an LLC. As we learned in Chapter 5, LLCs are initially financed by their members contributing cash, property or services. A member who contributes *cash* to the LLC acquires basis in the amount of the cash. A member who contributes *property,* is considered to have sold that property to the LLC. Unlike a typical sale of property, which would ordinarily require the member to report a gain or loss on the sale, applicable tax rules instead treat the member as making a nonreportable exchange of property for a membership interest. The member's basis in the property is transferred to the LLC so that, when the property is later sold, the amount and character of the gain or loss will be determined as if the member had sold the property.

Finally, a member who contributes *services* to an LLC may receive, in exchange, either a capital interest or a profits interest. Under applicable tax rules, such a member may need to report a capital interest as taxable income unless it is subject to a "substantial risk of forfeiture." By contrast, the receipt of a profits interest in an LLC is generally a tax-free event, unless its income stream can be valued because of its predictability. By contrast, a shareholder's contribution of services in exchange for stock is taxable.

Another advantage that LLCs offer over S corporations relates to the tax treatment of the respective owners upon their contribution of appreciated assets to the business. The term *appreciated assets* generally refers to property with (presumably as a result of a rise in market value) a fair market value that is greater than the property's adjusted basis. In S corporations, a shareholder who contributes appreciated property to the business in exchange for stock must recognize a taxable gain. A limited exception to this rule eliminates this tax only if the contributing shareholder owns at least 80 percent of the corporation's stock immediately after the transfer has been completed. By contrast, members of LLCs can generally contribute appreciated property to the business without incurring a tax because Subchapter K of the Internal Revenue Code does not require the recognition of gain on the appreciation. These tax-free transactions are available to any member of an LLC, not just those owning 80 percent or more of the business.

### Planning Tip 103

Since shareholders can only contribute assets to a corporation on a tax-free basis if they control 80 percent of the stock after the contribution, consider taking advantage of the relatively tax-free nature of a member's capital contributions in an LLC.

### Planning Tip 104

Consider how you can secure tax benefits by contributing appreciated assets to an LLC.

### Entrepreneurs in Action

John Smith and Mike Harris, members of Smith Restaurants, LLC, want to buy a state-of-the-art stove from Tina Reed that has a basis of $10,000 and a fair market value of $40,000. If Tina contributes the stove in exchange for a 20 percent interest in the LLC, she does not recognize any gain—and so pays no tax—on the transaction. If Smith and Harris had formed a corporation instead of an LLC, Tina may be liable for a capital gains tax on $30,000 ($40,000—$10,000)!

### Planning Tip 105

As in other businesses, neither LLCs nor their members are allowed deductions for startup costs incurred in forming the business (e.g., legal and accounting fees), selling membership interests and other such matters. Instead, discuss how these costs can be capitalized with your accountant.

# LLC Operations

An ongoing LLC business must determine its profits and losses each year so that its members can report their allocable share of such items and pay appropriate tax. Generally, members are free to allocate income, gains, losses, deductions and such other related items in any manner they find mutually agreeable. Typically, allocations are reflected in the LLC's operating agreement. Why is this flexibility in allocation useful? Let's consider an example. An LLC may look to one of its members to contribute a particular piece of property necessary for the business. The member may agree but only on the condition that all of the tax benefits generated by the property, such as depreciation, accrue only to his or her benefit. Not a problem using the LLC's special allocation provisions. Alternatively, members of an LLC may have varying tax and financial positions. One member may be able to use a deduction to help reduce his taxes while another member has otherwise managed to position herself for a tax refund. Instead of allocating the potential deduction to the two members on a pro-rata basis, the LLC can be used to allocate the deduction entirely to the member who can use it. The portion of the deduction that would otherwise have gone to the member expecting a refund is not wasted. Moreover, this member may now be in a position to barter for an alternative tax or other benefit that she can use! This flexibility is yet another advantage LLCs have over corporations, which require allocations of such items to be made on a pro-rata basis and cannot even pass their operational losses on for use by shareholders.

Notwithstanding an LLC's general flexibility to allocate tax items, there are certain limitations set forth in the Internal Revenue Code. Let's briefly review these limitations.

### Allocations Must Have Substantial Economic Effect

Perhaps the most important limitation imposed by the tax code on an LLC's use of special allocations of profits and losses to its members is the requirement that the allocations have "substantial economic effect." Generally, an economic effect is considered substantial if a reasonable possibility exists that the allocation will affect the income the members receive from the LLC, independent of tax consequences. An allocation is ordinarily found to have substantial economic effect if it is consistent with the allocation established for a member's financial interest. Thus, an allocation that favors one member should have a corresponding detrimental tax effect on other members. What are the consequences of a special allocation not having substantial economic effect? The allocation will be disregarded and a new allocation will be required to be made in accordance with the members' actual financial interests in the LLC.

Although this requirement does establish certain limits on an LLC's flexibility, there is still enormous opportunity to make special allocations *and* comply with the substantial economic effect requirement. By contrast, S corporations lack practically any flexibility because of the requirement for one class of stock. In an S corporation, each shareholder is allocated a pro-rata share of profits, losses and other tax items in proportion to stock ownership. Shareholders must generally share profits and losses in the same proportion. If allocations were specially made, the IRS would be forced to conclude that the S corporation had more than one class of stock, which would require a termination of the S election and result in tax treatment as a regular corporation. By contrast, the flexibility permitted in LLCs may seem extraordinary to individuals used to dealing with these S corporation limitations.

### Planning Tip 106

Consider how you can use an LLC's ability to flexibly allocate income, losses and other tax items to your advantage.

### Planning Tip 107

Although the tax code includes a number of "safe harbor" rules designed to ensure compliance with the substantial economic effect requirement, the easiest standard is to provide that the special allocation of profits, losses and other tax items shall follow the distribution of cash. Consider using this standard so that the allocations you make will have substantial economic effect.

## Entrepreneurs in Action

Although Tina Reed has only a 20 percent interest in Smith Restaurants, LLC, it may be possible to allocate 80 percent of the depreciation deductions attributable to an expensive stove she has contributed to the LLC. Without the ability to make special allocations, Tina's share of the deduction on this property would be 20 percent.

## *Basis Restrictions on a Member's Use of LLC Losses*

Assuming the LLC's allocations of tax losses have substantial economic effect, other hurdles may limit a member's ability to use such losses as current tax deductions. The tax code permits a member to deduct his or her allocable share of LLC losses only to the extent of his or her basis in the membership interest. *Basis* is simply a tax term that seeks to track a taxpayer's cost or investment in property. Why is a tracking device needed? First, it can establish the eligibility for a taxpayer to take a deduction (such as, for example, depreciation), which will reduce a tax payment otherwise due. Second, when certain property is sold, it may be subject to a capital gains tax on the portion of the sale price that exceeds the basis in the property sold or a capital loss deduction if the sale price is less than the basis in the property sold. As we see below, the higher the basis in property, the less tax due.

### Entrepreneurs in Action

#### Example 1: Smith Restaurants, LLC

| | | | |
|---|---|---|---|
| 1993 | $10,000 cash used to buy a new stove | | |
| | Original basis (cost) of stove | = | $10,000 |
| 1994 | LLC depreciates (reduces) value of stove by, say, $2,000 to reflect wear and tear and, ultimately, need to replace stove | | |
| | Adjusted basis of stove = $10,000 – 2,000) | = | $ 8,000 |
| 1995 | LLC invests $3,000 in capital improvements to enhance efficiency of stove | | |
| | Adjusted basis of stove = ($8,000 – $2,000*) + $3,000 | = | $ 9,000 |

*Annual depreciation for tax year.

1996      LLC sells stove with an adjusted basis of $9,000 to Billy Buyer for $10,000

| | | |
|---|---|---|
| Sale price | = | $10,000 |
| − Adjusted basis | = | 9,000 |
| Taxable gains | = | $ 1,000 |
| Income tax due | = | $ 280 (using 28 percent rate) |

**Example 2**

1995      Smith Restaurants, LLC sells stove with an adjusted basis of $6,000 to Billy Buyer for $10,000

| | | |
|---|---|---|
| Sale price | = | $10,000 |
| − Adjusted basis | = | 6,000 |
| Taxable gains | = | $ 4,000 |
| Income tax due | = | $ 4,120 (using 28 percent rate) |

**Observation.** The owner in Example 2 pays $3,840 more in capital gains tax than does the owner in Example 1 solely as a result of a difference in basis in the otherwise identical stoves.

### Asset Basis v. Ownership Basis

The foregoing example considered the basis treatment of a piece of property owned by a business (sometimes referred to as *inside basis*), not the basis an owner has in his or her ownership interest in a business (sometimes referred to as *outside basis*). The general theory behind the two types of basis is much the same. The aggregate of each owner's outside basis should equal the total inside basis of the property held by the business. A member who contributes cash or property to an LLC receives basis in his or her membership interest equal to the cash contributed plus the basis in any property also contributed. As discussed below, a member's basis also ordinarily includes his or her share of the LLC's debt if no member is personally liable for the repayment of such debt.

### Adjustments to a Member's Basis

From time to time, a member's interest in an LLC is adjusted to reflect changes in operations, liabilities and allocations. These changes will affect the basis in a member's ownership interest. Generally, a member's basis will be increased by (1) his or her share of income, (2) his or her share of liabilities and (3) his or her prior and current capital contributions. On the other hand, a member's basis is generally decreased by (1) both cash distributions and by the basis of any property distributed to the member, (2) the amount of a member's taxable losses in a tax year and (3) a member's share of nondeductible business expenditures. Although there are similarities in the rules governing the upward and downward adjustment of basis in S corporations and partnerships, important differences exist as well. Let's examine a few of these, because understanding them can help you appreciate certain additional benefits in using an LLC.

### Similarities to S Corporations

S corporations and LLCs have two important similarities in the manner in which basis is adjusted. First, in both entities, basis is increased if income is taxed to a shareholder or member but not distributed. So, for example, if an LLC with two members has $100,000 income that, instead of being distributed to the members, is reinvested in the business, the members' basis has been increased by $100,000.

The second similarity between S corporations and LLCs concerns distributions in excess of basis. In both business forms, any distribution to a shareholder or member that is in excess of the party's respective basis is taxable. For example, if an S corporation shareholder has a basis in stock of $100,000 and receives a distribution of $200,000, the tax law provides that the first $100,000 is a return of capital, and so is not taxable, and the next $100,000 is income and taxable to the shareholder. A similar tax result would be felt by a member who received an identical distribution from an LLC.

### Differences from S Corporations

Notwithstanding these similarities, there are important distinctions in the way basis is adjusted in S corporations and the way it is adjusted in LLCs. One distinction, which is based on the way the two entities treat debt, confers an additional advantage on LLCs over S corporations. In an S corporation, a shareholder's basis is not adjusted in the event the business incurs indebtedness. Perhaps surprisingly, the result does not change even if the shareholder personally guarantees the debt. By contrast, an LLC's liabilities can increase the basis of the members' LLC interests to the full extent of their allocable share of the debt of the business. Under applicable tax rules, when an LLC borrows money on a nonrecourse basis, the debt will create additional basis, which can be shared by the members. Since higher basis translates into lower tax, members of LLCs will be in a better position than shareholders of an S corporation in an otherwise identical situation.

Because of the LLC's treatment of nonrecourse debt as part of a member's basis, bank and other third-party financing can provide an attractive advantage to LLC members not available to S corporation shareholders. LLC members can potentially deduct more losses than simply the amount of their cash or other capital contribution to the business; they can also deduct losses up to the amount of their additional pro-rata share of the LLC's financing. Shareholders in S corporations, by contrast, can only deduct losses up to the amount of their cash or other capital contribution in the business; their basis is not increased by third-party financing. Moreover, a member of an LLC may be able to receive a distribution resulting from a refinancing on a tax-free basis while a distribution to an S corporation shareholder in a similar circumstance would generally be taxed. In order for an S corporation shareholder to increase his or her basis, is it possible for him or her to borrow money personally and then lend it to the corporation? (Remember, corporate debt does not increase a shareholder's basis, but personal debt does.) While this alternative may be possible, there are some inherent disadvantages with such a strategy. Perhaps most important, the shareholder will have personal liability for such debt instead of having the corporation bear responsibility for repayment. Additionally, the credit terms available to an individual may be less favorable than those available to a corporate borrower. Recourse debt is treated differently under the tax code and its complex rules should be considered with your adviser.

### Planning Tip 108

Consider how the use of debt in an LLC can improve your tax situation.

### Planning Tip 109

If a member has tax losses from LLC operations that cannot be used because he or she has no or insufficient basis, consider "carrying forward" the losses and using them as deductions in later years when additional basis in membership interests may be available.

## At-Risk Limitations

Even though an LLC's allocations meet the requirements for substantial economic effect noted above, and even though a member may have sufficient basis in his or her membership interest, a member's ability to currently deduct his or her allocable share of LLC losses may be restricted because of *at-risk* limitations. Under the tax code, a member of an LLC will be considered at risk for (1) the cash and adjusted basis of property that the member contributes to an LLC, (2) any loan that the member has personally guaranteed or for which he or she has pledged property as security for the loan (to the extent of the fair market value of such pledged property) and (3) most bank debt. Because of the limited liability protection otherwise offered to members of an LLC, the liabilities of an LLC are generally ignored in determining what a member has at risk.

**Planning Tip 110**

If you are unable to use a tax loss due to the at-risk rules, carry the loss forward and use it in a future year when your at-risk amount has been increased.

# Passive-Loss Limitations

Congress decided to establish yet another limit on a taxpayer's use of business losses as a deduction where the loss is generated by a passive activity. Essentially, Congress was eager to prevent a tax shelter investment from producing tax losses greater than the amount a taxpayer invested in the shelter. The solution it developed came in the form of what is commonly referred to as passive-loss rules. Basically, these rules provide that a taxpayer is precluded from deducting losses generated by certain passive activities in excess of income generated from such activities during a taxable year. When is an investment deemed *passive*? Under applicable Treasury regulations, losses are generally considered passive unless the investor can show one of the following:

1. He or she spent more than 500 hours a year working on behalf of the business.
2. He or she materially participated in the business for five of the preceding ten taxable years.
3. For certain professions, he or she materially participated for any three preceding years.

For example, a physician who invests in an apartment building will generally be able to deduct only losses from the real estate activity against the rental income or other similar passive income. Although precise applications of these rules in an LLC context have not yet been clarified by the IRS, a member of an LLC will, presumably, be subject to these rules and allocable losses will be deemed passive unless the member can demonstrate he or she meets one of the three requirements for material participation set forth above.

These rules suggest that an LLC may offer a tax advantage unavailable to limited partnerships. Specifically, a limited partner's role in a limited partnership is passive by definition; involvement in management would expose the limited partner to personal liability. Of course, the limited partner could seek to avoid the passive-loss limitation rules but relinquishing this limited liability protection to do so seems like a foolish choice. By contrast, a member of an LLC can avoid the passive loss limitations by meeting the material participation requirements set forth above and, at the same time, retain limited liability protection!

Moreover, LLCs offer other decided advantages over corporations with respect to the use and treatment of tax losses. For example, shareholders of C corporations are unable to take a personal deduction for a corporate loss. By contrast, because an LLC is a pass-through entity, its losses are passed directly through to its members, who can use such losses as income deductions.

### Planning Tip 111

Consider the possibility of avoiding passive-loss limitation rules by forming an LLC and meeting the material participation requirements of the tax code.

## Taxation of Distributions to LLC Members

When an LLC distributes cash or property to a member, the income tax consequences are determined by whether the distribution is either a "current" (i.e., non-liquidating) distribution or a liquidating distribution, which is made when a member completely terminates his or her interest in an LLC. A current distribution includes every other type of distribution. For example, an LLC's distribution of a member's share of current year earnings is considered a current distribution.

### Tax Consequences of Current Distributions

A current distribution of cash to a member of an LLC is generally a tax-free event unless the value of the distribution exceeds the member's basis in the business. If, instead of cash, the LLC distributes property, the member does not recognize a taxable gain or loss until he or she later disposes of the property.

An LLC offers more desirable tax treatment than does a corporation upon the distribution of cash or appreciated property to its owners. If a corporation distributes appreciated property to its shareholders, the corporation and shareholders recognize a capital gain to the extent that the fair market value of the property exceeds the shareholder's stock basis. Moreover, shareholders are generally unable to recognize a loss on the distribution of depreciated property. As noted above, however, distributions of identical property to LLC members are generally received free of income tax to the members. Further, a corporation's cash distributions to its shareholders are generally income taxable as dividends. By contrast, an LLC's distribution of cash to its members is tax free to the extent of each member's basis.

### Entrepreneurs in Action

Smith Restaurants, LLC, distributes $5,000 cash to both John and Mike. John's basis is $10,000 while Mike's basis is $1,000. John has no taxable gain while Mike has taxable gain in the amount of $4,000. John, Jr., who has a basis of $500, receives a distribution of property with a value of $1,000. John, Jr., also recognizes no taxable gain at the time of distribution although his basis in the property becomes $500. If he sells the property at a later date in excess of $500, he will then have a gain.

### Planning Tip 112

Consider how you can use an LLC to reduce or eliminate taxes on distributions to members.

## Tax Consequences of Liquidating Distributions

As noted above, a liquidating distribution is made to a member upon the complete termination of his or her membership interest in the LLC. Generally, such a distribution is tax free unless the amount of money distributed exceeds the member's basis.

A business is generally deemed to be completely liquidated when it ceases its operations as a going concern and its activities are limited to winding up its affairs, paying its debts and distributing any remaining assets to its owners. The tax cost of liquidating an LLC may be significantly less than that of liquidating a similar business that operated as a corporation. For example, when a C corporation is being liquidated, the corporation must recognize a capital gain when distributing appreciated assets to the extent the fair market value of the assets distributed exceeds the shareholder's adjusted basis in the property. The corporation then distributes assets to its shareholders, who also incur a gain to the extent the fair market value of the distributed property exceeds the adjusted basis in their shares. In effect, two levels of capital gains tax may be paid—one at the corporate level, another at the shareholder level.

By contrast, when an LLC is liquidated, its members do *not,* with limited exceptions, recognize any gain or loss on the distribution of property. Instead, the liquidation of the LLC is generally tax free. The members may be liable for a capital gains tax if the fair market value of the property they receive through the distribution exceeds their basis in the LLC upon a subsequent sale of that property. In short, use of an LLC instead of an S or regular corporation can help eliminate an entire level of additional tax.

### Entrepreneurs in Action

*Example 1.* John Smith has basis in Smith Restaurants, LLC, in the amount of $10,000. Upon his retirement, he receives a cash distribution in the amount of $8,000 and property with a fair market value of $1,000. John does not recognize a gain on this distribution.

*Example 2.* The same facts apply although John receives a cash distribution of $20,000 upon his retirement. John recognizes a gain of $10,000.

*Example 3.* The same facts apply although John receives a cash distribution of only $5,000. This time, John has a capital loss of $5,000.

### Taxation on Termination of LLCs

When there is a change in an LLC's capital or profits interests of 50 percent or more in any 12-month period, the LLC is deemed to be terminated for tax purposes. The LLC is considered to have distributed its assets to its members and, at the same time, the new members contribute assets back to the "new" LLC. When a member's interest terminates, the LLC can make an election under the tax code to "step up" (or increase) the inside basis of the LLC's assets to a fair market value of such assets. The opportunity to adjust a member's basis in its assets may be a significant benefit to the LLC or its members. This opportunity is not available to S corporations and their shareholders.

#### Entrepreneurs in Action

*Example 1.* John and Mike have formed an S corporation to operate their restaurant. They have a disagreement that, after months of negotiations, results in Mike selling his stock back to the corporation. Included in the redemption price is Mike's share of company receivables and fully depreciated equipment (i.e., equipment with a book value of zero). Ordinarily, Mike pays a capital gains tax on the sale of his stock. The corporation payment for the stock is treated as a nondeductible redemption.

*Example 2.* Everything is the same as above except that John and Mike formed an LLC. Upon his termination, Mike pays income tax on his share of receivables and depreciation recapture. In addition, the LLC could receive basis for Mike's receivables and the basis in the otherwise depreciated equipment is stepped up.

#### Planning Tip 113

A number of complex and potentially negative tax effects may result from the termination of an LLC, which should be considered with your adviser.

# Taxation upon Transfers of Membership Interests

A member who sells his or her membership interest in an LLC to another party generally recognizes a taxable gain or loss, which is measured by the difference between the member's basis in the interest and the amount of the sale price. The buyer of the membership interest ordinarily receives basis equal to the cash paid for the interest. If the buyer pays for the interest not with cash but with property, his or her initial basis is equal to the fair market value of such property. Special elections or circumstances can, of course, produce different tax results.

### Entrepreneurs in Action

John has a 50 percent interest in Smith Restaurants, LLC, with a basis of $10,000. He sells his interest to Howard Davis for $20,000 cash. John must recognize a taxable gain of $10,000 ($20,000 proceeds less $10,000 basis). Howard's basis in the interest is $20,000.

# Self-Employment Tax

Under the Self-Employment Contribution Act, a tax is imposed on "self-employment" income. The tax is a combination of a tax for old-age, survivor and disability insurance (12.40 percent) and hospital insurance (2.90 percent). In a recent private letter ruling, the IRS concluded that members of an LLC, which was classified as a partnership for income tax purposes, were subject to a self-employment tax. The members' shares of income (and loss) from the LLC were includable in computing each member's net earnings from self-employment. In this case, each member of the LLC was actively involved in the business. If the members are passive investors with no management responsibility, a good argument could be made that their distributions should not be subject to the self-employment tax. Indeed, under the tax code, a limited partner, who is essentially a passive investor, is not subject to a self-employment tax. In a proposed regulation, the IRS has taken the position that a member's net earnings from his or her share of an LLC's income or loss is generally subject to self-employment tax. An exception is established, however, if (1) a member is *not* a manager and (2) the LLC could have been formed as a limited partnership and, as so formed, the member would have qualified as a limited partner. In these situations, such members should not be subject to the self-employment tax. Whether the IRS will apply the self-employment tax to members who play a passive role in the LLC, however, remains to be determined.

### Planning Tip 114

Consider the possible application of a self-employment tax to your LLC income with your advisers.

## Taxation of Fringe Benefits

LLCs are free to provide certain qualified retirement and fringe benefits to their members, including, for example, adoption of a Keogh plan. Certain restrictions apply, which you should consider with your adviser. For example, if a member is not subject to the self-employment tax for the reasons set forth in the previous section, he or she may not be able to participate in a qualified benefits plan. Moreover, certain fringe benefits that are not generally taxable to employees of corporations may be taxable to members of LLCs because partners are not treated similarly to employees in such cases. These benefits may include group term life insurance, medical benefits and cafeteria plan benefits. You should consider this subject with your tax adviser.

## Taxation of One-Member LLCs

Some, but not all, of the LLC acts either expressly or impliedly authorize the formation of LLCs with only one member. How the IRS will tax one-member LLCs remains uncertain. Traditional partnership classification will likely be unavailable because a partnership, by definition, contemplates an association of two or more partners. As a result, a one-member LLC will likely be taxed as a sole proprietorship or as a corporation.

### Planning Tip 115

Because of the uncertain tax treatment of one-member LLCs, use of an alternative business form such as an S corporation may be preferred. Moreover, members of an LLC should consider including a provision in their operating agreement that the LLC will always have at least two members. Such an agreement could specify who would become a new member if one member in a two-member LLC dies, retires or otherwise withdraws.

# Miscellaneous Tax Accounting Rules

### LLCs May Use a Cash or Accrual Method

LLCs may be able to use either a cash basis or an accrual basis accounting method, but certain limitations to this rule may apply. For example, if the LLC is being used in connection with a registered securities offering, only the accrual method can be used. The flexibility to select either accounting method is an advantage to members of LLCs that is not available to shareholders of C corporations, who must use the accrual method of accounting.

### Selection of an LLC Tax Year

Applicable regulations provide that an LLC must select as a tax year the same tax year as is used by a majority of its members. If there is no majority interest taxable year, the tax year will be the same as a calendar year unless the LLC can convince the IRS that a legitimate business purpose justifies the selection of an alternative year.

### Tax Matters Partner

Any LLC with more than ten members is required to designate one of its members as a *tax matters partner*. This designee is responsible for, among other things, facilitating LLC tax audit proceedings in a manner that permits the IRS to review tax issues at the LLC level, instead of requiring the IRS to audit each individual partner. In a partnership, the tax matters partner is ordinarily the partner with the largest profits interest. Presumably, the member with the largest membership interest would also qualify.

### LLC Tax Returns

Like partnerships, LLCs must file an information tax return. Currently, there is no separate form for LLCs although, with their increasing popularity, such a form may be developed in the future. For the time being, LLCs should file their information return on IRS Form 1065 and check the box indicating that the return is being filed by an LLC. As with partnerships, LLCs will furnish their members with K-1 forms, which the members, in turn, will use when filing their individual tax returns.

## Private Letter Rulings

Because the LLC business form is in its infancy, a number of questions regarding its features have already arisen and more are certain to arise in the future. Many of these questions bear on whether an LLC, organized in a particular manner, will be classified as a partnership or a corporation for tax purposes. The IRS has established general procedures to obtain a determination on certain of these tax issues, including how it will characterize your LLC. Depending on the procedure you follow, the IRS determination may take the form of a private letter ruling, a determination letter or an information letter. Although these procedures can offer comfort when testing new planning techniques, they are complex and cumbersome. Consider using an attorney whenever seeking a ruling from the IRS.

### Planning Tip 116

The IRS has indicated that if a private letter ruling is desired on the classification of a new LLC as a partnership, the request should be made prior to filing the LLC's first tax return.

# CHAPTER 9

# Converting Your Existing Business to an LLC

OK! OK! You've gotten the message. An LLC is a good thing. You like its flexibility, its limited liability protection and its pass-through tax treatment. The only thing you don't like is that your existing business isn't an LLC! If you're about to establish a new business, you may want to skip this chapter. If, however, you own an established business and are thinking about whether to convert, how you can convert and the consequences of converting, read on! This chapter is for you.

## Converting Your Proprietorship to an LLC

If you've been operating your business as a sole proprietorship and would like to secure limited liability, you have two potential options. The first option would be to form an LLC with a second member (perhaps a spouse or child) and contribute the proprietorship's assets to an LLC. The other option would be to form an S corporation, which, although generally less attractive then LLCs, can be owned by one shareholder.

# Converting Your Partnership to an LLC

Existing general partnerships may find it desirable to convert to LLCs to secure increased protection from personal liability for partnership obligations. Existing limited partnerships may find it particularly desirable to convert to LLCs because of the increased managerial roles allowed individuals whose status is converted from limited partner to member. Other reasons for converting a partnership to an LLC include the continuation of pass-through tax treatment, flexibility in structuring ownership interests, lack of tax on conversion (see below) and ease of the conversion process.

These advantages should be available to a partnership converting to an LLC without having to incur any material disadvantages. Let's examine the conversion process and the principal tax consequences of making a conversion.

## The Conversion Process Is Easy To Follow

The conversion of a general or limited partnership to an LLC is generally straightforward and can be accomplished with a minimal effort. The partnership must first choose the state in which it would like to organize. As discussed in Chapter 2, a state with a bulletproof or flexible LLC act can be selected. Bulletproof acts ensure partnership tax treatment but have less flexibility. Flexible LLC acts have more structuring flexibility but, with sloppy draftsmanship, can permit the formation of LLCs with a majority of corporate characteristics and, so, be taxed as a corporation.

Once this initial decision is made, you may wish to evaluate reasonable alternative state LLC acts to find the one most consistent with your objectives. For example, what are the state's consent requirements for the admission of new members? What are its provisions regarding management by members and/or managers?

Once the state is chosen, find out about your selected jurisdiction's conversion process, which is spelled out in its LLC act. In most cases, the process is relatively easy and will only require filing articles of organization for a new LLC along with a certificate of merger documenting the conversion (or merger) of the existing business to an LLC.

### Planning Tip 117

A sample certificate of merger is included in Appendix A. You and your attorney may be able to refine this sample to meet your state's requirements.

### Planning Tip 118

As in the formation of a new LLC, most state LLC acts require the payment of certain minimal filing fees and the publication of a notice in an appropriate newspaper, which gives the public notice of the conversion. Check your state's requirements.

## No Tax on Conversion

General and limited partnerships can, with limited exceptions, be converted to LLCs without any adverse tax consequences. Several private letter rulings from the IRS help explain why such favorable tax consequences exist. For example, in Revenue Ruling 84-52, the IRS concluded that a general partnership's conversion into a limited partnership was the equivalent of the general partners exchanging their partnership interests for interests in the limited partnership. The IRS, which concluded in this case that the conversion would not be treated as a termination of the general partnership for tax purposes, determined that such an exchange would not result in a taxable gain unless the distribution from the general partnership exceeded the partner's outside basis.

The IRS has already relied on Revenue Ruling 84-52 in several private letter rulings involving the conversion of both general and limited partnerships to LLCs to confirm the availability of a tax-free conversion. The tax-free nature of a conversion will depend on the LLC qualifying as a partnership for federal income tax purposes and the continuation of the old partnership business after the conversion.

A variety of factors could potentially affect the tax consequences of a conversion or the basis in membership interests following conversion. For example, changes in allocable ownership interest shares, the elimination of personal liability for existing debt obligations and heavy leverage are a few of the relevant factors that may trap the unwary. A tax may also be imposed if a general partnership with partners who have recourse debt (i.e., partners have personal liability for repayment of the debt) is converted to an LLC, and the debt is repaid and replaced with nonrecourse debt (no member is liable for the repayment of the debt).

In most cases, the *state tax* treatment of a partnership converting to an LLC will match the *federal tax* treatment accorded by the IRS. As a result, a state tax should not ordinarily be incurred on a conversion.

### Planning Tip 119

Before converting your business to an LLC, consider your particular situation with counsel.

### Planning Tip 120

Because of the generally available tax-free conversion process from partnership to LLC, if you own a general partnership in one of the few remaining states without LLC legislation and would like to secure limited liability protection, you may wish to consider converting your general partnership to a limited partnership. If (or when) your state adopts LLC legislation, a tax-free conversion may then be easily accomplished.

### Conversion Mechanics

The mechanical steps by which a partnership is converted may be spelled out in your state LLC's law. Regardless which route is taken, the IRS can be expected to treat the transaction as an essentially tax-free constructive contribution of a partnership assets and liabilities to an LLC. The LLC should be treated as a continuation of the former partnership. A few of the routes that may be available are the following:

*Asset Contribution.* In an asset contribution, the partnership contributes its assets and liabilities to an LLC in exchange for most of the membership interests in a new LLC. A second member is initially issued the remaining membership interest so that the LLC meets the two-member requirement. The membership interests are then distributed to the former partners in the same proportion as they held their partnership interests. The second member's interest can then be liquidated.

*Partnership Dissolution.* A partnership following this conversion route would first dissolve the partnership and distribute all of the assets and liabilities of the business to the partners in accordance with their partnership interests. The partners then contribute these same assets and liabilities to a new LLC, in exchange for the LLC's membership interests.

*Straight Conversion.* In a straight conversion, the partners simply amend their partnership agreement into an operating agreement. The partners form an LLC by filing articles of organization and, thereafter, sell or assign all of the partnership's assets and liabilities to the LLC in exchange for membership interests.

*Ownership Contribution.* In this conversion route, all of the partners in a partnership contribute their partnership interests to a newly formed LLC. In exchange for contributing their ownership interests, the LLC issues the partners all of its membership interests. The partnership is typically dissolved and, upon dissolution, its assets and liabilities are assigned to the LLC.

# Converting Your Corporation to an LLC

Although it is possible for existing corporations to convert to LLCs, current LLC acts and applicable tax rules make it unlikely that many will do so. First, only some state acts expressly permit the direct merger of a corporation into an LLC. Instead, a more convoluted route ordinarily needs to be followed. Perhaps the corporation could sell all of its assets to an LLC in exchange for membership interest. More likely, the corporation would liquidate and the shareholders could contribute the remaining assets to the LLC in exchange for membership interests. Even in states that specifically authorize the merger of a corporation into an LLC, the Internal Revenue Code does not contemplate that the merger will be tax free. Instead, legal precedent suggests that a conversion of this sort will be treated as if the corporation transferred its assets to the LLC in exchange for a membership interest. After such an exchange, the LLC's membership interest is deemed to be distributed to the corporation's shareholders as part of a complete liquidation.

In many instances, a capital gain or loss will have to be recognized to the extent the fair market value of the distributed assets exceeds or falls short of the shareholders' basis in the property. A corporation that owns a substantial amount of appreciated assets will therefore recognize significant income on conversion. Although this tax consequence also applies to S corporations, there may be partially ameliorating circumstances. For example, the gain recognized on liquidation of S corporation assets increases the basis in shareholders' stock. That increase can later be used by the member (former shareholder) to reduce otherwise applicable taxable gain when a liquidating distribution is paid to the shareholder.

### Planning Tip 121

If a corporation is deemed to liquidate its assets as part of the conversion, assets that may not be included on the corporation's books will also be "liquidated." For example, a corporation may have significant goodwill that is not recorded. Be careful to consider how the liquidation and deemed distribution of such assets may increase what may already be significant gain from just the liquidation of assets on the books!

### Planning Tip 122

It may be possible to merge a corporation into an LLC as a tax-free reorganization if the LLC has a majority of corporate characteristics and, so, is taxed as a corporation. Although the LLC would not offer the benefit of pass-through taxation, its other features may be more attractive to you than the corporate form. You should discuss this option with your advisers.

### Planning Tip 123

The basis in a shareholder's stock is "stepped-up" upon his or her death to the fair market value of the stock. Since, by definition, the basis would then equal fair market value, there would be neither a capital gain nor a capital loss if the corporation were liquidated. Accordingly, following the death of a sole or substantial shareholder of a corporation, you may wish to reconsider converting your business into an LLC.

### Planning Tip 124

Although it may be difficult for existing corporations to convert to LLCs, new operations could, if shareholders agree, be "diverted" to new LLCs. Consider this aggressive strategy only upon advice of counsel.

### Planning Tip 125

If a corporation identifies a prospective joint venture opportunity, consider making the corporation's shareholders members of a new LLC to pursue the opportunity instead of the corporation itself. This will permit the shareholders to secure pass-through tax treatment on the joint venture earnings while retaining their limited liability protection.

### Planning Tip 126

Owners of corporations who would like to avoid the double level of tax they are currently paying but are concerned about the high cost of converting to an LLC should consider, instead, the possibility of electing S corporation status. If you satisfy the eligibility requirements, such an election could represent an improvement on your current status with a lower conversion cost.

## *The Effect of Conversion*

Following the conversion of an existing business into an LLC, all of the rights, powers, property, debts, obligations and other things belonging to that business thereafter become the property or are otherwise vested with the LLC. Nevertheless, rights of pre-existing creditors are ordinarily preserved, and they may enforce their obligations as if no conversion had taken place. In other words, a debtor may not avoid a debt obligation by simply converting his or her business.

### Planning Tip 127

Some LLC acts provide specific procedures by which partners or shareholders who prefer not to convert for some reason can be bought out on specified terms. If applicable, consider how you can use such mechanisms to prevent dissenting owners from holding up a conversion in order to extract an unfair advantage for themselves.

# CHAPTER 10

# Dissolving Your LLC

Dissolution is the process by which members of an LLC end their relationship with each other. A variety of circumstances or events may precipitate a dissolution. We will consider the most common of those below. Unless the members agree to continue the business following an event of dissolution, the affairs of the LLC are wound up, obligations satisfied and assets liquidated and distributed to the members. When the required procedures have been completed and the business formally terminated by the filing of a certificate of dissolution with the secretary of state or designated official, the process is complete. In this chapter, we explore the causes and mechanics of dissolution as well as how, if desired, two or more members can continue the business.

## Causes of Dissolution

An LLC may terminate for any number of reasons. Members are free to specify when their LLC will be dissolved by including appropriate terms and conditions in their articles of organization or operating agreement. Unless otherwise agreed to, a default provision in most LLC acts requires dissolution in the event of a member's death, incapacity, bankruptcy, expulsion or withdrawal from the LLC. In order to avoid possessing the corporate characteristic of continuity of life (and, perhaps, risk being taxed as a corporation), members often include in their articles of organization or operating agreements a provision that their LLC shall be dissolved upon the *first* to occur of the following:

1. The latest date provided in the articles of organization
2. At the time of the happening of events specified in the operating agreement
3. The vote or written consent of the members

LLC acts specify the required number of members, or percentage of interest they hold, to approve of a dissolution by vote or written consent. The members may be able to change such standards in their articles of organization or operating agreement and provide for higher or lower consent requirements. Events that may cause dissolution are addressed differently by states in their LLC acts. Flexible LLC acts permit members a great degree of latitude to structure their events of dissolution. In these states it may be possible to provide for dissolution only if one trigger event occurs. In other states, an LLC that does not provide for dissolution in the traditional events noted above may be deemed to have continuity of life and, so, risk being taxed as a corporation. Until more guidance is available, the safe approach is to include all these events as causes of dissolution in your operating agreement.

### Planning Tip 128

If your LLC has voting and nonvoting members, you may wish to specify whether nonvoting members should, notwithstanding their general status, have a vote on the decision to dissolve.

### Planning Tip 129

Consider how to tailor events of dissolution to best address your situation.

## *Use of a Dissolution Agreement*

It is common for problems to occur when a business is being dissolved, regardless of whether it will be terminated or whether remaining members have agreed to continue the business. Some of the matters often included in such an agreement are the following:

- Which members shall participate in the dissolution process
- Any limits on the authority of one or more members during the process
- Dispute resolution mechanisms
- The manner in which assets should be liquidated
- The manner in which creditors' claims should be reviewed and, if legitimate, satisfied

- The manner in which any assets that remain after satisfying creditors should be distributed to the members

### Planning Tip 130

Consider using a dissolution agreement upon the dissolution of an LLC.

## Judicial Dissolution

In addition to specified events of dissolution provided by agreement of members or by statute, LLC acts also authorize designated courts within their jurisdiction to dissolve LLCs by judicial order. The grounds for judicial dissolution tend to mirror those set forth for the judicial dissolution of a corporation: illegality, fraud, waste, violation of public policy and the impracticability of continuing the operations of the business.

In some states, an application for judicial dissolution can only be made by a member; in other states, a member or manager can make the application; in still other states, any person who is adversely affected by specified conduct or events involving an LLC may be able to petition for judicial dissolution.

## Continuing the Business Following Dissolution

Following an event of dissolution, the remaining members can decide to continue the business. All of the state acts contemplate that a business may be continued upon agreement of an LLCs members, but requirements regarding the necessary level of agreement vary. In order to ensure a lack of continuity of life, a number of states took the position that unanimous consent of the membership is required. The IRS has recently indicated that a simple consent of a majority in interest of the members to continue the business would not cause continuity of life to exist. The term *majority in interest* has recently been defined by the IRS to mean the remaining members who hold both a majority of the profits and capital interests in an LLC. As a result, some states have reduced their default consent requirement or, alternatively, retained the unanimous default requirement but permit LLC members to agree that the consent of a simple majority of members will be sufficient.

States also impose related requirements that the members must meet to continue an LLC. For example, some states require that at least one member remain in the LLC after the dissolution; others require at least two members to remain; still other states have no such requirement. Some states specify that an LLC can be continued only if the right to do so had been included in the company's articles of organization or operating agreement. In some states, the decision to continue must even be reached within a specified period following an event of dissolution.

Because of the practical problems in seeking at least majority consent to continue a business upon the occurrence of an event of dissolution, some LLCs have required their members to consent in advance to continue the LLC if an event of dissolution should occur. The use of such advance consent agreements has prompted authorities to ask whether they create continuity of life in such businesses. To date, there is no clear answer to the question. Analysis suggests that such an agreement may not cause an LLC to possess this corporate characteristic as long as each member may choose to breach the agreement, that is, retains the power to dissolve the LLC. The fact that a breach may give rise to a lawsuit should be irrelevant from a tax planning perspective.

### Planning Tip 131

Consider the standards for continuing an LLC upon member agreement in your state. If possible, establish specific standards for continuation that are tailored for your situation.

### Planning Tip 132

If an agreement to continue the business is reached, consider preparing a written continuation agreement to specify the mechanics of the process. Such an agreement could, for example, include provisions addressing the following subjects:

- How a withdrawing member's interest in the LLC should be valued
- Establishment of a funding mechanism to compensate withdrawing member (which, like traditional buy-sell agreements, may contemplate the use of life insurance to provide liquidity)
- Confidentiality and noncompetition provisions
- The extent that continuing members assume predissolution liabilities of the LLC

### Planning Tip 133

Consider using agreements in which members consent in advance of a dissolution event to continue the LLC only upon advice of counsel or after securing a private letter ruling.

### Planning Tip 134

Because of the possible difficulties in trying to continue an LLC following an event of dissolution, consider whether this is a corporate characteristic that is desirable for your LLC to possess. As long as the only other corporate characteristic possessed is limited liability (presumably), the LLC should be taxed as a partnership.

## Winding Up and Distributions upon Dissolution

If the members of an LLC choose not to continue their business, then the affairs of the business must be wound up. The winding up process encompasses all that activity between the occurrence of a dissolution event and the formal termination of the business. The assets of the business are liquidated in (hopefully) the most economical fashion and the proceeds are then distributed, first to creditors and then, if any proceeds are left, to the members as provided by the terms of the operating agreement or, if none, by the applicable default provision in the state LLC act. A common default provision stipulates that upon the winding up of the company, the assets be distributed as follows:

- To creditors, including members who are creditors, to the extent permitted by law, in satisfaction of liabilities of the company
- Except as provided in the operating agreement, to members and former members in satisfaction of liabilities for certain enumerated distributions
- Except as provided in the operating agreement, to members, first, for return of their capital contributions, to the extent not previously returned, and thereafter, in the proportions in which the members share in distributions

## Powers of Members or Managers after Dissolution

An LLC that is being wound down and terminated cannot pursue new business opportunities. Instead, the assets must be liquidated as soon as is reasonably practicable. The LLC acts contain a variety of default provisions concerning who is responsible for actually liquidating the assets and winding up the LLC's affairs. Some states authorize the managers to perform this role or, if none, the members. Some states specify that those members who were not responsible for the dissolution shall be in charge of the winding up process. Still other states permit either members or managers to wind up an LLC. Most states permit members the opportunity to vary these otherwise applicable default provisions upon agreement by the members. Because such agreement may be difficult or impossible to reach at the time of dissolution, it is usually a good idea to specify who will be responsible for winding up your LLC in your operating agreement.

Some states have acknowledged that circumstances may create an unsatisfactory result if any or specified members or managers (whether designated by agreement or by default) are left in charge of the winding up process. In these states, it is possible to petition an appropriate court for a judicial dissolution. Upon order of the court, a trustee can then be appointed to wind up the affairs of the LLC. Although the appointment of a trustee could increase the administrative expense, it helps ensure a fair and orderly liquidation process.

### Planning Tip 135

Consider seeking the appointment of a trustee upon the dissolution of an LLC.

## Articles of Dissolution

The dissolution of the company is effected by filing a certificate of dissolution with the secretary of state or other designated official (the same official who accepts articles of organization for filing). When this certificate has been accepted, an LLC's articles of organization will be cancelled. The purpose of filing the certificate is to provide notice to the public that the LLC has been terminated so that the public won't unwisely extend credit or supplies, or perform services, for the business. The filing process varies slightly from state to state. Some states require a separate notice of the LLC's intent to dissolve; other states specify the formal termination of the business upon the filing of articles of dissolution. In other states, termination is effective upon the issuance of a certificate of cancellation. Many states require a fee to accompany the articles of dissolution. If remaining members of an LLC choose to continue the business following an event of dissolution, and the filing of articles of dissolution, some states require these members to file articles of continuation. You will need to refer to the particular requirements and standards set forth in your state's LLC act. A sample form of articles of dissolution, that you may wish to use in consultation with your attorney, is attached as Appendix A.

### Planning Tip 136

Check your LLC act to determine applicable filing requirements associated with the dissolution and/or continuation of your LLC.

# CHAPTER 11

# Is a Limited Liability Partnership for You?

When enacting their new LLC acts, a number of state legislatures also created a related new form of partnership known as a limited liability partnership (LLP). In many cases, the creation of LLPs was accomplished by simply amending existing state partnership laws. In this chapter, we briefly examine the general character of LLPs, how they can be used, how they are formed and how they compare with both general partnerships and LLCs. As with the LLC acts, there is no uniform LLP act. Each state's act is unique. Accordingly, the discussion is general in nature and you should consider your state's statutory requirements if you choose to form and operate an LLP.

### Planning Tip 137

The states that have enacted LLP legislation to date are Arizona, Connecticut, Delaware, Illinois, Iowa, Kansas, Kentucky, Louisiana, Maryland, Minnesota, New York, North Carolina, Ohio, South Carolina, Texas, Utah and Virginia, as well as the District of Columbia. Consider the merits of forming an LLP under the law of one of these jurisdictions.

# Definition of an LLP

As we learned in Chapter 1, in a general partnership, each general partner is liable for not only the debts and obligations of the business, but for *all* of the wrongful or tortious conduct of any partner, employee or agent of the partnership. As partnerships expand in size, often establishing multistate offices, relationships among partners become less personal and more formal. An increasing lack of personal contact makes it difficult or impossible to keep tabs on what the partners are doing or how well they are doing it.

An LLP is designed to reduce liability exposure to individuals for the wrongful acts of their partners. This special form of partnership is one which has made a statutory election to provide a certain degree of protection to its partners from liability caused by the wrongful or tortious conduct of other partners, employees or agents of the partnership. The only exception to this protection is that a partner continues to be responsible for his or her own wrongful or tortious conduct or for similar conduct caused by a person under his direct supervision or control. The LLP continues, of course, to be responsible for its ordinary business obligations. Because a partnership requires at least two owners, an LLP is generally unavailable to sole practitioners.

### Planning Tip 138

Consider using an LLP to reduce the exposure to liability claims caused by lack of contact or familiarity within a partnership.

## Limited Liability Protection Available

While the scope of the limited liability protection may vary from state to state, LLPs generally provide their partners with protection not only from damages caused by the wrongful conduct of other partners but from any debts, obligations or other liabilities incurred by the LLP as well. As a result, partners are generally *not* responsible for the LLP's failure to pay its creditors or, in some states, an LLP's breach of contract. Although partners continue to be responsible for their own acts of malpractice, as well as those caused by individuals under their direct supervision, malpractice insurance continues to be available to provide a safety net in case such claims are asserted. Indeed, many LLP acts provide that an LLC must either carry malpractice insurance, segregate cash or secure a letter of credit in a designated amount so that a malpractice victim will have a minimum level of assets to seek recovery against.

Some observers have suggested that the limited liability protection offered by LLPs may be broad enough to even insulate partners from claims for employment, age, sex, race or religious discrimination. At this time, however, there is insufficient case precedent to confirm this suggestion. The safer approach is to assume that personal liability for such conduct in the absence of otherwise applicable legal defenses potentially exists.

### Planning Tip 139

Partners in an LLP can specify that certain partners are liable for some or all of the LLP's debts, obligations or liabilities. Consider defining different levels or tiers of partners who have varying rights and obligations, as well as varying levels of compensation. Consider the specific limited liability protection offered by your LLP law.

## LLPs Can Be Used By Professionals

Unlike LLC acts, which often preclude their use by professionals, LLP acts generally permit duly authorized professionals to operate as LLPs. Designated professions typically include doctors, lawyers, accountants, veterinarians, engineers, architects and psychologists. These professions will benefit by enactment of this new law since it represents an improvement over existing alternative forms of business in which such professionals can operate. For example, a group of professionals that would like to secure limited liability protection for business debts and obligations could elect to operate as a PC. Aside from having eligibility requirements that are sometimes hard to meet, PCs are taxed as regular corporations, resulting in double-level taxation of the PC's income! Although a PC can elect S corporation status, additional eligibility requirements further limit its use. For example, a business with more than 35 shareholders would be required to operate as a regular corporation. Because LLPs have no comparable restrictions, professionals will likely find their use preferable to available alternatives.

### Planning Tip 140

States may have varying requirements on the need for each partner in an LLP to be a duly licensed professional authorized to provide such services as those offered by the LLP. In some cases, as long as at least one partner is authorized to render a professional service, the partnership can register as an LLP. In other cases, each partner must be a duly authorized professional. Check your state's requirements.

# Forming an LLP

LLPs are formed in much the same manner as are LLCs. Although state procedures may vary slightly because of the lack of uniform law, LLPs are typically formed by the filing of a registration statement with the secretary of state or other designated official for the state in which the business is being formed. The statement may require information such as the following:

- The name of the LLP
- The address of the principal office
- The designation of an agent for service of process
- The effective date of registration
- The profession to be practiced by the partners

Also, like LLCs, a filing fee must be paid at the time of registration. In some states, smaller annual or biannual fees are required thereafter. Many states also have a publication requirement, which mandates that an actual copy of the LLP's registration statement or a brief summary of its contents be published in a designated newspaper for a specified period of time. Be certain to check your state's particular requirements.

## Naming Your LLP

States require that an LLP be identified as such in its name. As a result, these states generally require the name of the business (which must meet other applicable professional ethical requirements for use of names by a partnership) is to be followed by one of the following or similar designations: (1) limited liability partnership, (2) registered limited liability partnership, (3) LLP or (4) RLLP.

# Tax Treatment of LLPs

The federal tax treatment of LLPs should also mirror that accorded to LLCs. Thus, as long as the LLP lacks a majority of corporate characteristics (i.e., limited liability, continuity of life, centralization of management or free transferability of interests), the entity should be taxed as a partnership. Existing partnerships that convert into LLPs should be deemed to continue their partnership operations and retain their pre-existing tax treatment for federal income tax purposes. As with LLCs, state tax treatment may vary and an LLP may be required to pay an annual fee based on the number of its partners.

# Treatment of LLPs in Foreign States

Because this is a relatively new form of business with little precedent available, it is difficult to predict exactly how an LLP that operates in a jurisdiction other than that in which it is formed will be treated. A number of assumptions, however, can be made. First, an LLP that operates in another jurisdiction with its own LLP statute should be recognized as a legitimate entity and the limited liability protection of its partners respected. This conclusion should be particularly true if such foreign jurisdiction(s) have special provisions permitting the qualification of foreign LLPs to do business in their states.

Treatment of LLPs in states that don't currently have their own LLP acts is less certain. Partners can argue, of course, that their entity should be respected and their limited liability protection recognized on the basis of the full faith and credit clause of the U.S. Constitution and the principle of "comity," which provides that courts in one state should honor the laws of another state out of respect and courtesy. How, ultimately, LLPs will be treated in non-LLP states remains to be determined.

# LLPs versus LLCs

Lets take a minute to compare how LLPs stack up against LLCs. First, the similarities. Both entities (if properly structured) are able to secure the benefit of pass-through partnership tax treatment and avoid an entity-level tax. Both entities offer a high degree of flexibility in structuring the management of the business as well as the allocation of profits, income, losses and other tax and financial attributes.

What's the biggest difference in the two forms? LLPs offer a different degree of limited liability protection for their partners than LLCs do for their members. LLCs are generally structured so that no member is personally liable for debts or obligations of the business. LLPs, on the other hand, provide similar protection from contractual debts and obligations of the business, as well as from the professional malpractice of other partners in the business. LLPs do not, however, insulate a partner from claims arising out of his or her own malpractice or that caused by another individual in the firm under his or her direct supervision. Of course, as noted above, many state laws do not permit certain professional partnerships to use the LLC form. For such professionals, the LLP form could present a significant new planning opportunity that should be considered in conjunction with professional advice. Many individuals who prefer to operate in a more traditional "corporate" form may prefer to use an LLC. For those more comfortable using a traditional "partnership" form, the LLP may be the form of choice.

## Planning Tip 141

Consider the various differences between an LLC and an LLP with your attorney before making your selection.

# CHAPTER 12

# The Dynamic LLC Opportunity State by State

It is an exciting time! The rapid enactment of LLC legislation promises to reshape the business landscape. Strangers to LLCs today will be using them tomorrow. How the historical forms of business weather the assault on their citadels of prominence in the business world remains to be seen. Only time will tell if limited partnerships and S corporations continue to serve entrepreneurs to the same degree they have in the past. Only one thing is certain. LLCs have arrived and they are here to stay! The many advantages LLCs confer on their owners make it a desirable option to consider. I hope that this book has explained how many of these advantages may be able to help you address your business needs.

What follows in this chapter is a state-by-state chart, breaking down the title of the LLC act, the title of the organizational document, address and phone number and filing fee. Because LLC legislation has been enacted by each state separately, consider reviewing a copy of your state's actual LLC act or contacting the appropriate official in your state to determine local filing requirements. The attached chart was prepared to help facilitate this process. If you're still stuck, feel free to give me a call. If I can, I'd love to help.

| State | Title of LLC Act | Title of Organizational Document | Address and Phone Number (Subject to Change) | Filing Fee (Subject to Change) |
|---|---|---|---|---|
| Alabama | Alabama Code Title 10, Chap. 12 §27-31-A-1 et seq. | Articles of Organization | Probate Judge in County where initial registered office is located | $40 State Fee $35 Probate Court Fee |
| Alaska | Alaska Stat. §10.50 et seq. | Articles of Organization | Dept. of Commerce and Economic Dev. Pouch D Juneau, AK 99811 907-465-2530 | $350 |
| Arizona | Arizona Rev. Stat. Ann §29-60 et seq. | Articles of Organization | Arizona Corporations Commission 1200 W. Washington St. Phoenix, AZ 85007 602-542-3076 | $50 |
| Arkansas | Arkansas Code Ann. §4-32-101 et seq. | Articles of Organization | Secretary of State Corporation Dept. State Capitol Bldg. Little Rock, AR 72201 501-682-5151 | $50 |
| California | California Bus. & Prof. Code §17000 et seq. | Articles of Organization | Secretary of State Corporate Filings 1230 J. St. Sacramento, CA 95814 916-445-7205 | $80 |
| Colorado | Colorado Rev. Stat. §7-80-101 et seq. | Articles of Organization | Secretary of State 1560 Broadway Denver, CO 80202 303-894-2200 | $50 |
| Connecticut | 1993 Conn. Pub. Acts No. 93-267, 94-217 Ch. 267 | Articles of Organization | Secretary of State 30 Trinity St. Hartford, CT 06106 203-566-8574 | $60 |
| Delaware | Del. Code Ann. Tit. 6, §18-101, et seq. | Certificate of Formation | Secretary of State Division of Corporations P.O. Box 898 Dover, DE 19903 302-739-3073 | $50 |

| State | Title of LLC Act | Title of Organizational Document | Address and Phone Number (Subject to Change) | Filing Fee (Subject to Change) |
|---|---|---|---|---|
| District of Columbia | DC Code §29 -1301 et seq. | Articles of Organization | Dept. of Consumer & Regulatory Affairs 614 H. St. N.W. Washington, DC 20001 202-727-7287 | $100 |
| Florida | Florida Stat. Ch. 608.40 et seq. | Articles of Organization | Secretary of State Tallahassee, FL 32314 904-487-6052 | $87.50 min. |
| Georgia | Georgia Code Ann. §14-11-100 et seq. | Articles of Organization | Secretary of State Business Serv. & Regulations Suite 315, West Tower 2 Martin Luther King Jr. Drive, SE Atlanta, GA 30334 404-656-2817 | $75 |
| Hawaii | No LLC laws | | NA | NA |
| Idaho | Idaho Code §53-601 et seq. | Articles of Organization | Secretary of State Division of Corporations State House Boise, ID 83720 208-334-2300 | $100 (typed) $120 (not typed) |
| Illinois | 805 ILCS §180-1-1 et seq. | Articles of Organization | Secretary of State LLC Division Springfield, IL 62756 217-524-8008 | $500 |
| Indiana | Indiana Code §23-18-1-1 et seq. | Articles of Organization | Secretary of State Corporations Division State House Indianapolis, IN 46204 317-232-6585 | $90 |
| Iowa | Iowa Code §490A. 100 et seq. | Articles of Organization | Secretary of State Corporation Division Des Moines, IA 50319 515-281-5204 | $50 |

| State | Title of LLC Act | Title of Organizational Document | Address and Phone Number (Subject to Change) | Filing Fee (Subject to Change) |
|-------|------------------|----------------------------------|-----------------------------------------------|--------------------------------|
| Kansas | Kansas Stat. Ann. §17-7601 et seq. | Articles of Organization | Secretary of State Corporation Division Topeka, KS 66612 913-296-2236 | $150 |
| Kentucky | Kentucky Rev. Stat. Ann. §275.001 et seq. | Articles of Organization | Secretary of State State Capitol Bldg. Frankfort, KY 40602 502-564-2848 | $40 |
| Louisiana | Louisiana Rev. Stat. Ann. §12:1301 et seq. | Articles of Organization | Secretary of State Corporations Division P.O. Box 94125 Baton Rouge, LA 70809 504-925-4704 | $60 |
| Maine | Maine Rev. Stat. Ann. Tit. 13, §601 et seq. | Articles of Organization | Secretary of State Corporation & UCC Division Augusta, ME 04333 207-289-4195 | $250 |
| Maryland | Maryland Ann. Code Art. 4A, §4A-101 et seq. | Articles of Organization | State Dept. of Assessments & Taxation 301 W. Preston St. Baltimore, MD 21201 410-225-1330 | $50 |
| Massachusetts | No LLC Law | NA | NA | NA |
| Michigan | MSL §450.4101 et seq. | Articles of Organization | Michigan Dept. of Commerce, Corporation & Securities Bureau Box 30054 Lansing, MI 48909 517-373-0493 | $50 |
| Minnesota | Minn. Stat. §322B.01 et seq. | Articles of Organization | Secretary of State Corporation Division 180 State Office Bldg. St. Paul, MN 55155 612-296-2803 | $135 |

| State | Title of LLC Act | Title of Organizational Document | Address and Phone Number (Subject to Change) | Filing Fee (Subject to Change) |
|-------|------------------|----------------------------------|----------------------------------------------|--------------------------------|
| Mississippi | Miss. Code Ann. §29-101 et seq. | Certificate of Formation | Secretary of State P.O. Box 136 Jackson, MS 39205 601-359-1350 | $50 |
| Missouri | Mo. Rev. Stat. §347.010 et seq. | Articles of Organization | Secretary of State Jefferson City, MO 65301 314-751-2827 | $100 |
| Montana | Mont. Code Ann. §35-8-101 et seq. | Articles of Organization | Secretary of State State Capitol Helena, MT 59260 406-444-3665 | $70 |
| Nebraska | Neb. Rev. Stat. §21-2601 et seq. | Articles of Organization | Secretary of State Corporation Division 2304 State Capitol Bldg. Lincoln, NE 68509 402-471-4079 | $100 min. |
| Nevada | Nev. Rev. Stat. §86.011 et seq. | Articles of Organization | Secretary of State Corporation Division Carson City, NV 89710 702-687-5203 | $85 |
| New Hampshire | N.H. Rev. Stat. Ann. §304-C:1 et seq. | Certificate of Formation | Secretary of State Corporation Division 204 State House Concord, NH 03301 603-271-3246 | $35 |
| New Jersey | N.J. Rev. Stat §42.2 B-1 et seq. | Certificate of Formation | New Jersey Dept. of State Commercial Recording Bureau Corporate Filing Section CN-308 Trenton, NJ 08625 609-530-6400 | $100 |

| State | Title of LLC Act | Title of Organizational Document | Address and Phone Number (Subject to Change) | Filing Fee (Subject to Change) |
|---|---|---|---|---|
| New Mexico | N.M. Stat. Ann. §53-19-1 et seq. | Articles of Organization | State Corporation Commission Corporation & Franchise Tax Depts. P.O. Drawer 1269 Santa Fe, NM 87504 505-827-4504 | $50 |
| New York | N.Y. Consl. Law, Ch. 34, §101-114 et seq. | Articles of Organization | New York State Division of Corporations 162 Washington Ave. Albany, NY 12231 518-474-4750 | $200 |
| North Carolina | N.C. Gen. Stat. §57C-1-01 et seq. | Articles of Organization | Secretary of State Corporations Division 300 N. Salisbury St. Raleigh, NC 27603 919-733-4201 | $100 |
| North Dakota | N.D. Cent Code §10-32-01 et seq. | Articles of Organization | Secretary of State Division of Corporations Bismarck, ND 58505 701-224-2900 | $125 |
| Ohio | Ohio Rev. Code Ann. §1705.01 et seq. | Articles of Organization | Secretary of State Division of Corporations State Office Tower, 30 E. Broad St. Columbus, OH 43226 614-466-3910 | $85 |
| Oklahoma | Okla. Stat. Ann. Tit. 18 §2000 et seq. | Articles of Organization | Secretary of State Room 101 State Capitol Bldg. Oklahoma City, OK 73105 405-521-3911 | $100 |
| Oregon | OR Rev. Stat. §631.001 et seq. | Articles of Organization | Secretary of State Corporation Commissioner 255 Capitol N.E. Salem, OR 97310 503-986-2200 | $40 |

| State | Title of LLC Act | Title of Organizational Document | Address and Phone Number (Subject to Change) | Filing Fee (Subject to Change) |
|---|---|---|---|---|
| Pennsylvania | 15 PACSA §8901 et seq. | Certificate of Organization | Commonwealth of Penn. Corporation Bureau Harrisburg, PA 17120 717-787-1057 | $100 |
| Rhode Island | R.I. Gen. Laws §7-16-1 et seq. | Articles of Organization | Secretary of State 100 N. Main St. Providence, RI 02903 401-277-3040 | $150 |
| South Carolina | S.C. Code Ann. §33-43-101 et seq. | Articles of Organization | Secretary of State Box 11350 Columbia, SC 29201 803-758-2744 | $110 |
| South Dakota | S.D. Code. Laws Ann. §47-34-1 et seq. | Articles of Organization | Secretary of State State Capitol Pierre, SD 57501 604-773-4845 | $50 min. |
| Tennessee | Tenn. Code Ann. §48A-1-101 et seq. | Articles of Organization | Secretary of State Corporation Division Nashville, TN 37219 615-741-2286 | $300 min. |
| Texas | Tex. Rev. Civ. Stat. Ann. Art. 153,800, Art. 1.01 et seq. | Articles of Organization | Secretary of State Corporation Division Sam Houston State Office Bldg. Austin, TX 78711 512-463-5555 | $200 |
| Utah | Utah Code Ann. §48-2b-101 et seq. | Articles of Organization | Dept. of Commerce Corporation Division 160 East 300 South P.O. Box 45801 Salt Lake City, UT 84145 801-530-4849 | $75 |
| Vermont | No LLC Law | NA | NA | NA |

| State | Title of LLC Act | Title of Organizational Document | Address and Phone Number (Subject to Change) | Filing Fee (Subject to Change) |
|-------|------------------|----------------------------------|----------------------------------------------|--------------------------------|
| Virginia | VA Code Ann. §13.1-1000 et seq. | Articles of Organization | Clerk of the State Corporation Commission Box 1197 Richmond, VA 23209 804-371-9733 | $100 |
| Washington | 1994 Wash. Laws Ch. 211 Rev. Code Wash. Ch. 25.15 et seq. | Certificate of Formation | Secretary of State Corporations Division Republic Bldg. 2nd Floor 505 E. Union Olympia, WA 98504 206-753-7115 | $175 |
| West Virginia | W.VA Code §31-1A-1 et seq. | Articles of Organization | Secretary of State Corporation Division State Capitol Bldg. Charleston, WV 25305 304-558-8000 | Same as corporations. |
| Wisconsin | Wis. Stat. §183.0102 et seq. | Articles of Organization | Secretary of State Corporation Division State Capitol Bldg. Madison, WI 53702 608-266-3590 | $90 |
| Wyoming | Wyo. Stat. §17-15-101 et seq. | Articles of Organization | Secretary of State Division of Corporations Capitol Bldg. Cheyenne, WY 82002 307-777-7311 | $50 min. |

# Appendix A:
## Sample Forms for Creating and Operating an LLC

The forms that follow are provided as examples only. They may not be suitable for use in your situation! Legal counsel should be consulted to prepare appropriate forms that comply with applicable laws and that reflect the actual agreement of the parties to the transaction.

# ARTICLES OF ORGANIZATION

## ARTICLES OF ORGANIZATION OF SMITH RESTAURANTS, LLC

Under Section _____ of the (State) Limited Liability Company Law

FIRST:           The name of the limited liability company is: Smith Restaurants, LLC.

SECOND:       The county within this state in which the office of the limited liability company is to be located is: _____.

THIRD:         (optional) The latest date on which the limited liability company is to dissolve is: _____.

FOURTH:      The secretary of state is designated as agent of the limited liability company upon whom process against it may be served. The post office address to which the secretary of state shall mail a copy of any process against the limited liability company served upon him or her is: _____.

FIFTH:         (optional) The name and street address within this state of the registered agent of the limited liability company upon whom and at which process against the limited liability company can be served is: 1234 Main Street, Yourtown, USA.

SIXTH:         (optional) The future effective date of the Articles of Organization (if not effective upon filing), is: _____.

SEVENTH:    The limited liability company is to be managed by one manager.

EIGHTH:     [The articles may include any other provisions not inconsistent with law.]

IN WITNESS WHEREOF, this certificate has been subscribed this 15th day of March, 1995, by the undersigned who affirms that the statements made herein are true under penalties of perjury.

X _____     John Smith, Organizer _____

(signature)                          (name and capacity of signer)

# APPLICATION TO RESERVE NAME

APPLICATION BY JOHN SMITH FOR RESERVATION OF NAME
UNDER (STATE) LIMITED LIABILITY COMPANY LAW

APPLICANT'S NAME AND
ADDRESS:

John Smith

123 Hamburger Way, Anytown, USA

NAME TO BE RESERVED:

Smith Restaurants, LLC

RESERVATION IS INTENDED FOR (Check One):

New domestic limited liability company:                                   X

Foreign limited liability company intending to apply for
authority to do business in _____ State:                    _____

Change of name of an existing limited liability company:      _____

Foreign limited liability company intending to apply for
authority to do business in _____ State whose name is
not available for use in _____ State:                         _____

X _____              John Smith, Manager _____

Signature of applicant,                       (name and capacity of signer)
applicant's attorney or agent
(if attorney or agent, so specify)

# CERTIFICATE OF AMENDMENT TO ARTICLES OF ORGANIZATION

CERTIFICATE OF AMENDMENT

TO THE

ARTICLES OF ORGANIZATION

OF

Smith Resturants, LLC

Under Section _____ of the (State) Limited Liability Company Law

FIRST: The name of the limited liability company is: Smith Restaurants, LLC.

SECOND: The date of the filing of the articles of organization is: March 15, 1995.

THIRD: The amendments affected by this certificate of amendment are as follows: (set forth each amendment in an independent subparagraph).

Example (A) Paragraph "seventh" of the Articles of Organization dealing with the management of the LLC is hereby amended to read as follows: "The limited liability company is to be managed by two managers."

IN WITNESS WHEREOF, this certificate has been subscribed this 28th day of Aguust, 1995, by the undersigned who affirms that the statements made herein are true under the penalties of perjury.

X _____
(signature)

John Smith, Manager
(name and capacity of signer)
Smith Restaurants, LLC

# OPERATING AGREEMENT

OPERATING AGREEMENT
OF
SMITH RESTAURANTS, LLC

THIS OPERATING AGREEMENT of Smith Restaurants, LLC (the "Company") dated March 15, 1995, is made by and between JOHN SMITH ("Smith") and MIKE HARRIS ("Harris") as members (collectively the "Members").

The parties hereto do hereby agree as follows:

## ARTICLE I. FORMATION

1. **ORGANIZATION.** The parties agree that Smith will act as an organizer to form a limited liability company (the "Company") by filing with your State Secretary (the "Secretary") Articles of Organization (the "Articles") pursuant to the State Limited Liability Company Act (together with all amendments thereto, the "Act").

2. **NAME.** The name of the Company is Smith Restaurants, LLC.

3. **PRINCIPAL PLACE OF BUSINESS.** The principal place of business of the Company shall be located at 1234 Main Street, Yourtown, USA. The Company may establish other places of business as the Manager (as hereinafter defined) deems appropriate.

4. **TERM.** The Company shall be dissolved and its affairs wound up in accordance with the Act and this Agreement thirty (30) years from the date of filing of the Articles with the Secretary, unless the term is extended by amendment to this Agreement and the Articles, or unless the Company is sooner dissolved and its affairs wound up in accordance with the Act and this Agreement.

5. **PURPOSE.** The Company is formed solely for the purpose of developing and operating restaurants.

6. **LIMITATION OF ACTIVITIES AND ACTION.** The scope of the activities and business of the Company and the actions to be taken by the Members or Manager are limited to those reasonably necessary to accomplish the Purpose and nothing herein

is intended or shall be construed to constitute permission for any Member or Manager to pursue any other purpose or activity on behalf of the Company.

7. **REGISTERED AGENT.** The Company's registered agent shall be the AAA Service Company, having a registered office at 10 Busystreet, State Capitol.

## ARTICLE II. MEMBERS

1. **INITIAL MEMBERS.** The initial Members of the Company, are Smith, who shall own a 60 percent membership interest, and Harris, who shall own a 40 percent membership interest (the "Initial Members"). Their addresses are set forth on the exhibit attached to this Agreement.

2. **ADDITIONAL MEMBERS.** Additional members (the "Additional Members") may be admitted upon the unanimous written agreement of the Initial Members. Unless otherwise agreed to by the Initial Members, such members shall acquire not more than a total of 30 percent of the membership interest in the LLC. The Initial Members and Additional Members, if any, are referred to collectively herein as the "Members."

3. **BOOKS AND RECORDS; INSPECTION.** The Company shall maintain all of its books and records at its principal place of business, which any Member may inspect during normal business hours.

4. **LIMITATION OF LIABILITY.** No Member shall be personally liable for any debt, obligation or other liability of the Company, except as otherwise required by this Agreement, the Act or any other applicable law.

5. **CONFLICTS OF INTEREST.** Members shall be free to enter into any transaction that may be considered to be competitive with the business of the Company, except that no member shall be permitted to work for, or own more than a 5 percent interest in, any other restaurant business that specializes in the sale of hamburgers.

## ARTICLE III. MANAGEMENT

1. **MANAGEMENT.** The Company shall be managed by John Smith in the capacity of a manager (the "Manager") who shall have and be subject to all of the duties and liabilities of a Manager contained in this Agreement, the Act and any other applicable law. The members further agree that Smith shall serve as the Manager for an initial ten-year term, unless sooner terminated as provided herein.

**2. AUTHORITY TO BIND THE COMPANY.** The Manager shall have exclusive authority to act on behalf of, and to bind, the Company.

**3. BANK AND INVESTMENT ACCOUNTS.** The Manager shall be responsible for maintaining such bank and investment accounts as he deems appropriate, in his sole discretion. Only the Manager shall be authorized to withdraw funds form such accounts and/or make investment decisions with respect thereto.

**4. MANAGER SHALL ACT IN GOOD FAITH.** The Manager shall perform his duties in good faith, in the manner he reasonably believes to be in the best interests of the Company and with such degree of care as an ordinarily prudent person in a similar position would use under like circumstances. If the Manager so performs his duties, he shall have no liability by reason of being or having been a Manager and shall not be liable to the Company or to any Member for any loss or damage sustained by the Company. Notwithstanding the foregoing, the Manager shall be liable to the Company for any loss or damage that is a direct and proximate result of the gross negligence or willful misconduct of the Manager.

**5. DUTY TO COMPANY; CONFLICTS OF INTEREST.** The Manager shall not be required to devote his exclusive efforts to the management of the Company as his sole and exclusive function and may have other business interests other than those relating to the Company; provided, however, that without the prior unanimous written consent of the Members, the Manager shall not be entitled to enter into transactions that may be considered to be competitive with the business of the Company.

**6. INDEMNIFICATION.** The Company shall indemnify and hold harmless the Manager for all costs, losses, liabilities and damages paid or incurred by such Manager in the performance of his duties under this Agreement, to the fullest extent permitted by the laws of the State, unless caused by a Manager's violation of his obligation or duty to act in good faith pursuant to Section 4 of this Article.

**7. SALARIES.** The salaries and other compensation of the Manager shall be fixed from time to time by the unanimous vote or written consent of the Members.

**8. OFFICERS.** The Manager hereby designates the following persons as the initial officers of the Company:

| | |
|---|---|
| President | John Smith |
| Vice President | Mike Harris |
| Secretary | Mike Harris |
| Treasurer | John Smith |

Each officer shall have only those powers and authority as are expressly delegated to such officer by the Manager. Any officer may be removed, with or without cause, by the Manager at any time. Any number of offices may be held by the same individual. The salaries and other compensation of the officers, if any, shall be fixed exclusively by the Manager.

**9. REMOVAL.** The Manager may be removed and replaced only for a material breach of this Agreement, for the gross negligence or willful misconduct in discharging his duties, or upon the unanimous consent of the Members.

**10. RESIGNATION.** The Manager may resign his position at any time upon giving not less than 60 days, prior written notice to the Members of his intent to resign.

## ARTICLE IV. MEETINGS OF MEMBERS

**1. ANNUAL MEETING.** The annual meeting of the Members shall be held on such date and at such time as shall be determined by the unanimous agreement of the Members.

**2. SPECIAL MEETINGS.** Special meetings of the Members, for any purpose or purposes, may be called by any Manager or any Member in accordance with the provisions of Article IV, paragraph 4.

**3. PLACE OF MEETINGS.** Meetings of the Members shall be held at the principal place of business of the Company, unless there is unanimous agreement of the Members to meet elsewhere.

**4. NOTICE OF MEETINGS; WAIVER.** Written notice stating the place, day and hour of the annual or special meeting, by or at whose direction the meeting is being called and the purpose for which the meeting is being called, shall be delivered to each Member no fewer than five nor more than thirty days before the date of the meeting. Necessity for such notice can be dispensed with in the event a member either (a) submits a signed waiver of the notice requirement or (b) attends the meeting without protesting the lack of notice prior to the conclusion of the meeting.

**5. QUORUM.** Each of the Initial Members must be present at any meeting of the Members in order to have a properly constituted quorum. In the event that additional members have joined the Company, at least two-thirds of the Members must be present to have a properly constituted quorum.

**6. MANNER OF ACTING.** If a quorum is present at any meeting of the Members, the unanimous vote of the Members shall be necessary for the Members to take any action.

**7. PROXIES.** Members may attend or vote at any meeting of the Members by proxy.

**8. ACTION BY WRITTEN CONSENT.** Whenever the Members are required or permitted to take any action by vote, such action may be taken without a meeting, prior notice or a vote, if a consent in writing setting forth the action so taken is signed by all of the Members.

## ARTICLE V. CAPITAL CONTRIBUTIONS

**1. INITIAL CONTRIBUTIONS.** The Initial Members shall each make the following initial contributions to the capital of the Company (the "Initial Contributions"):

| | | |
|---|---|---|
| SMITH: | (A) | $60,000 in cash; and |
| | (B) | property consisting of the undeveloped land at 123 Hamburger Way (as more fully described in the legal description attached hereto) and two stoves. |
| HARRIS: | (A) | $40,000 in cash; |
| | (B) | management construction services as described in the attached summary; and |
| | (C) | professional style stove. |

**2. ADDITIONAL CONTRIBUTIONS.** From time to time, each Member shall make such additional Capital Contributions as they may unanimously agree upon to further the interests of the Company (the "Additional Contributions"). The Initial Contributions and Additional Contributions are referred to collectively herein as "Capital Contributions."

**3. CAPITAL ACCOUNTS.** A capital account (a "Capital Account") shall be maintained for each Member reflecting their Initial Contribution, increased by the value of Additional Contribution made by such Member and by allocation to such Member of

Net Profits (as hereinafter defined), and decreased by the value of Distributions (as hereinafter defined) to such Member and allocation to such Member of Net Losses (as hereinafter defined).

**4. DEFICIT CAPITAL ACCOUNT.** Each Member shall be fully liable to the Company at all times to restore any deficit balance in its Capital Account.

**5. INTEREST ON AND RETURN OF CAPITAL CONTRIBUTIONS.** No Member shall be entitled to earn any interest on any Capital Contributions, and may only receive a return of his Capital Contributions if all the debt, liabilities and obligations of the Company have been paid or satisfied or, in the sole discretion of the Managers, the property of the Company is sufficient to pay them.

## ARTICLE VI. ALLOCATIONS AND DISTRIBUTIONS

**1. ALLOCATIONS OF PROFITS AND LOSSES.** The Net Profits, defined herein as the income and gains of the Company determined in accordance with generally accepted accounting principals ("GAAP") consistently applied under the accrual method of accounting on the federal income tax return of the Company, and the Net Losses, defined herein as the losses and deductions of the Company determined in accordance with GAAP consistently applied under the accrual method of accounting on the federal income tax return of the Company, shall be allocated to each Member in accordance with their membership interests established pursuant to Article II, paragraph 1.

**2. DISTRIBUTIONS; OFFSET.** The Manager may, from time to time, in his discretion, make distributions to the Members pro rata in proportion to their respective membership interests ("Distributions"); provided, however, that the Company shall be required to offset all amounts owing to the Company by a Member against any Distribution to be made to such Member.

**3. LIMITATION UPON DISTRIBUTIONS.** No Distribution shall be declared and paid unless, after such Distribution is made, the assets of the Company are in excess of all liabilities.

## ARTICLE VII. TAXES

**1. TAX RETURNS.** The Manager shall cause to be timely prepared and filed all necessary federal and state income tax returns for the Company, and each Member shall cooperate in furnishing to the Manager all information relating to the Company reasonably necessary with respect thereto. The Manager shall make such elections permitted under the Internal Revenue Code which he deems to be in the best interest of the Members.

# ARTICLE VIII. TRANSFERABILITY

**1. GENERAL.** No Member shall gift, sell, assign, pledge, hypothecate, exchange or otherwise transfer to another person any portion of its membership interest without the prior unanimous written consent of all of the other Members, which consent shall not be unreasonably withheld. Notwithstanding the foregoing, transfers to children of Members shall not require the consent of the other Members.

**2. TRANSFEREE'S INTEREST.** No person acquiring a membership interest pursuant to this Article shall become a Member unless such person agrees to become a party and executes this Agreement.

# ARTICLE IX. DISPUTE RESOLUTION

In the event of a substantial dispute between the Members, the attorney for the Company shall designate an arbitrator and the dispute shall be submitted to that arbitrator. The arbitrator shall be authorized to render a decision to resolve the dispute that is binding on the members. The arbitrator's decision shall be nonappealable.

# ARTICLE X. DISSOLUTION

**1. DISSOLUTION.** The Company shall be dissolved and its affairs shall be wound up upon the first to occur of the following:

(a) The latest date on which the Company is to dissolve, if any, set forth in the Articles of Organization;

(b) The unanimous vote or written consent of all of the Members;

(c) The bankruptcy, death, dissolution, expulsion, incapacity or withdrawal of any Member or the occurrence of any other event that terminates the continued membership of any Member, unless within one hundred eighty (180) days after such event, the Company is continued by the unanimous vote or written consent of all of the remaining Members;

(d) A material breach of this Agreement by any Member, unless the non-breaching Members elect not to dissolve the Company; or

(e) The entry of a decree of judicial dissolution under the Act.

2. **VOLUNTARY WITHDRAWAL.** Any member can withdraw as a member of the Company upon not less than ninety (90) days' written notice to the other member. In the event of such withdrawal, a distribution shall not be required to be made until one hundred eighty (180) days from the date of withdrawal.

3. **WINDING UP.** Upon the dissolution of the Company, the Manager shall, in the name and on behalf of the Company, take all actions reasonably necessary to wind up the Company pursuant to the Act. If, however, the Company's dissolution has been caused by the Manager, Mike Harris, and any other non-Manager Members shall be responsible for taking such action.

4. **ARTICLES OF DISSOLUTION.** Within ninety (90) days following the dissolution and the commencement of winding up of the Company, or at any other time that there are no Members, articles of dissolution shall be filed by the Manager with the Secretary of State in accordance with the Act.

5. **TERMINATION.** Upon completion of the dissolution and winding up of the Company, the Company shall be deemed terminated.

### ARTICLE XI. GENERAL PROVISIONS

1. **NOTICES.** Any notice, demand or other communication required or permitted to be given pursuant to this Agreement (a "Notice") shall be deemed to have been given, if hand delivered, when delivered personally to the party or an executive officer of the party to whom such Notice is directed, or if mailed, three business days after the date on which it was deposited in a regularly maintained receptacle for the deposit of United States mail, by registered or certified mail, postage prepaid, addressed to the party or an executive officer of the party to whom such Notice is directed.

2. **AMENDMENTS.** This Agreement contains the entire agreement by and among the Members with respect to the subject matter hereof and may only be amended in a writing duly executed by all Members.

3. **HEADINGS.** The headings in this Agreement are for convenience of reference only and shall not be used to interpret any provision of this Agreement.

4. **WAIVER.** No failure of a Member to exercise, or delay by a Member in exercising, any right or remedy under this Agreement shall constitute a waiver of such right or remedy. No waiver by a Member of any such right or remedy under this Agreement shall be effective unless made in a writing duly executed by such Member and specifically referring to each such right or remedy being waived.

5. **SEVERABILITY.** Whenever possible, each provision of this Agreement shall be interpreted in such a manner as to be effective and valid under applicable law. However, if any provision of this Agreement shall be held to be prohibited by or invalid under such law, it shall be deemed modified to conform to the minimum requirements of such law or, if for any reason it is not deemed so modified, it shall be prohibited or invalid only to the extent of such prohibition or invalidity without the remainder thereof or any other such provision being prohibited or invalid.

6. **BINDING.** This Agreement and all provisions hereof shall be binding upon and inure to the benefit of the parties hereto and their respective successors, permitted assigns and transferees.

7. **COUNTERPARTS.** This Agreement may be executed in two or more counterparts, each of which shall be deemed an original.

8. **GOVERNING LAW.** This Agreement shall be governed by, and interpreted and construed in accordance with, the laws of your State.

IN WITNESS WHEREOF, the parties hereto have executed this Agreement as of the date first above written.

X _____
John Smith

X _____
Mike Harris

# CERTIFICATE OF MERGER (LLC SURVIVING)

## CERTIFICATE OF CONVERSION OF (PARTNERSHIP/LIMITED PARTNERSHIP) TO A LIMITED LIABILITY COMPANY

Under Section _____ of Your State Limited Liability Company Law

FIRST: The (partnership/limited partnership) was, in accordance with the provisions of the (State) Limited Liability Company law, duly converted to a limited liability company.

SECOND: The name of the partnership was: Smith and Smith.

THIRD: The name of the limited liability company is: Smith Restaurants, LLC.

FOURTH: The county within this state in which the office of the limited liability company is to be located is:

_____.

FIFTH: (optional) The latest date on which the limited liability company is to dissolve is: _____.

SIXTH: The Secretary of State is designated as the agent of the limited liability company upon whom process against it may be served. The post office address within or without this state to which the Secretary of State shall mail a copy of process against the limited liability company served upon him or her is:

_____.

SEVENTH: (Optional) The name and street address within this state of the registered agent of the limited liability company upon whom and at which process against the limited liability company can be served is:

_____.

EIGHTH: The limited liability company is to be managed by: one manager.

NINTH: The articles may include any other provisions not inconsistent with law.

IN WITNESS WHEREOF, this Certificate has been subscribed this 15th day of March, 1995, by the undersigned who affirms that the statements made herein are true under the penalties of perjury.

_____     Joh Smith, Manager
(signature)                         (name and capacity of signer)
                                       Smith Restaurants, LLC

# APPLICATION OF FOREIGN LLC FOR AUTHORITY TO DO BUSINESS

## APPLICATION FOR AUTHORITY

### OF

### Smith Restaurants, LLC

Under Section _____ of the (Foreign State) Limited Liability Company Law

FIRST:    The name of the limited liability company is: Smith Restaurants, LLC.

SECOND:   The jurisdiction of the limited liability company is: Home State. The date of its organization is: March 15, 1995.

THIRD:    The county within this state in which the office of the limited liability company is to be located is: foreign county, foreign state.

FOURTH:   The secretary of state is designated as agent of the limited liability company upon whom process against it may be served. The post office address within this state to which the secretary of state shall mail a copy of any process served against him or her is:

_____.

FIFTH:    (optional) The name and street address within this state of the registered agent of the limited liability company upon whom and at which process against the limited liability company can be served is:

_____.

SIXTH:    [statement setting forth the address of the office required to be maintained in the jurisdiction of its formation by the laws of that jurisdiction.]

SEVENTH:  Smith Restaurants, LLC is in existence in its jurisdiction of formation at the time of the filing of this application.

EIGHTH:     The name and address of the authorized officer of the limited liability company in the jurisdiction of its formation is John Smith, 123 Main Street, Hometown, His State.

IN WITNESS WHEREOF, this Certificate has been subscribed this 15th day of March, 1995, by the undersigned who affirms that the statements made herein are true under the penalties of perjury.

_____
(signature)


_____
(name and capacity of signer)

# ARTICLES OF DISSOLUTION

ARTICLES OF DISSOLUTION

OF

SMITH RESTAURANTS, LLC.

Under Section _____ of the (State) Limited Liability Company Law

FIRST:        The name of the limited liability company is: Smith Restaurants, LLC.

SECOND:       The date of the filing of the articles of organization and any subsequent amendment thereto or restatement thereof is as follows:
              _____.

THIRD:        The event giving rise to the filing of the articles of dissolution is the death of a member, John Smith.

FOURTH:       The effective date of termination is March 15, 1996.

FIFTH:        All of the debts and obligations of the LLC have now been paid. [Not required in all states.]

SIXTH:        All remaining property of the LLC, after payment of the debts and obligations of the business, has not been distributed. [Not required in all states.]

SEVENTH:      There are no lawsuits pending against the LLC. [Not required in all states.]

EIGHTH:       A notice of termination was sent by registered mail to each creditor of the LLC. [Not required in all states.]

NINTH:        The name and address of the member responsible for winding up the affairs of the business is Mike Harris, 1001 Milkyshake Way, Your Town, USA. [Not required in all states.]

IN WITNESS WHEREOF, this Certificate has been subscribed this _____ day of
_____, 19____, by the undersigned who affirms that the statements
made herein are true under the penalties of perjury.


_____
(signature)


_____
(name and capacity of signer)

# Appendix B:
## Comparison of Legal Entity Formations for Your Business

| Feature | General Partnership | Limited Partnership | S Corporation | LLC |
|---|---|---|---|---|
| Owner liability for business obligations | Yes | Yes for general partners | No | No |
| Ability to create different types of ownership interest | Yes | Yes | No | Yes |
| Restrictions on ownership eligibility | No | No | Yes | No |
| Limit of number of owners | No | No | Yes (35) | No (although 2 members is suggested minimum) |
| Ability to affiliate with other businesses | Yes | Yes | Limited | Yes |
| Management participation | No restrictions | Limited partners may lose limited liability for participating | No restrictions | No restrictions |
| Property distribution | Nontaxable | Nontaxable | Dividend (taxable) | Nontaxable |

# Index